Guide to the Superior Hiking Trail

Linking people with nature by footpath
along Lake Superior's North Shore

Guide to the
Superior Hiking Trail

Linking people with nature by footpath
along Lake Superior's North Shore

Edited by Andrew Slade
Ridgeline Press
1993

Guide to the Superior Hiking Trail

Copyright © 1993 Ridgeline Press

Printed in the United States of America
by McNaughton & Gunn, Inc.
First printing May 1993

Cover and text design: Sally Rauschenfels
Cover photo: Jay Steinke
Title page photo: Sam Cook

*Although the editors and publisher have researched all sources to ensure
the accuracy and completeness of the information contained in this
book, we assume no responsibility for errors, inaccuracies,
omissions or any inconsistency herein.*

ISBN: 0-9636598-0-4

Printed on recycled paper:
85% recycled fiber, 10% postconsumer waste
with soy ink

The Superior Hiking Trail

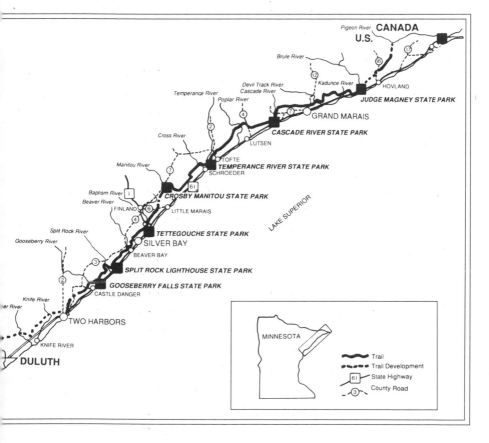

See an eagle, flush a grouse. Rest in a cool cathedral of pine, shiver atop windswept vistas of Lake Superior. Behold rushing inland rivers, find a moss garden and nap in a field of spring wildflowers. Explore this magnificent landscape shaped by the greatest lake.

for Tom Peterson and Mark Wester,
the heart and soul of the Superior Hiking Trail

Acknowledgements

Many thanks to all who helped make this book happen.

Photography: Jay Steinke, cover photo and Sam Cook, title page photo.

Project Coordinator: Nancy Hylden.

Trail Correspondents: Bill Anderson, Jill Dalbacka, Ron Wolff, Bunter Knowles, Don Schlossnagle, Jim Erickson, Ann Russ, Andrew Slade, Ruth Hiland, Karen Hanson, Miriam Graff, Bob Kotz, Bob Fox, Scott Beattie, Rudi Hargesheimer and Heidi Rigelman.

Field Checkers: Mike Anderson, Jim Erickson, Dave Geist, Rudi Hargesheimer, John Kohlstedt, Dick McDermott, Heidi Rigelman, Dick and Ella Slade, Anne and Peter Heegaard, Marilyn Vig, Andrew Slade, Bill Dryborough and Ted Tonkinson.

Contributing Writers: Deb Shubat, Nancy Hylden, John Green, Lee Radzak, Andrew Slade, Rudi Hargesheimer, Catherine Long, John Kohlstedt, Jeanne Daniels, Anne McKinsey, Cindy Johnson-Groh, Janet Green and Tricia Ryan.

Maps: Rudi Hargesheimer and Tom Peterson.

Book Production and Proofreading: Catherine Long, Tricia Ryan, Judy Gibbs, Kevin Roalson, Anne McKinsey, Rudi Hargesheimer, Tom Peterson, Kathy Hermes, Nancy Hylden, Jack Morris, Mark Wester and Sally Rauschenfels.

Additional Support: Christie's, Minnesota Power, H.T. Klatzky and Associates, Inc. and Colorworks Graphics, Inc.

Made possible in part through the generous donations of Bill Hursh and Potlatch Corporation.

Foreword

What I remember best is squatting on a shoulder of rock, gazing out at the Poplar River Valley. The valley was lush and green and rolled on forever. Down the middle of it meandered the river itself, a reflection of horseshoe bends flowing cool and blue through the lowlands.

I was hot and sweaty from a morning on the trail, and I don't know how long I sat there. I couldn't tell you what I thought about, other than that it was one of the finest places I've ever shed a pack and let the breeze glide over my skin.

Doubtless hundreds of hikers have had the same feeling at a hundred different places along the Superior Hiking Trail.

It is that good.

We owe a large debt to the visionaries who conceived this trail and to Tom Peterson, who must have worn out several pairs of boots choosing its route. It is difficult to hike any distance on the trail without emerging in awe of Peterson's genius and dedication.

And now we have Andrew Slade and a whole crew of other volunteers to thank for this mile-by-mile companion piece to the trail itself. It was a book begging to be written, but which was going to require the spirit of a naturalist and the research of a scientist.

The book's production team, with the help of geologists, botanists, ornithologists, historians and camping experts, has given us a compendium of information about the Superior Hiking Trail. The book's format is hiker-friendly. Its detail is complete. And it fits in a backpack.

This book can help you park your car, arrange a shuttle, find water or find a camp. It'll tell you where you're likely to see a moose or to see Isle Royale, where you're treading in the voyageurs' footsteps and why the rock fractures the way it does along the Split Rock River.

The information in this guide will not weigh you down. It will answer a lot of your questions and free you to get on with the walking.

And maybe one day you'll find yourself doing what I was doing that July morning, what backpacking guru Colin Fletcher calls "sitting on a peak and thinking of nothing at all except perhaps that it is a wonderful thing to sit on a peak and think of nothing at all."

Good reading. Happy walking.

— SAM COOK

Contents

The Superior Hiking Trail:
Mile-by-Mile Descriptions

History of the Superior Hiking Trail

The Superior Hiking Trail was conceived in the mid-1980's as a long-distance footpath, modeled after the Appalachian Trail and other long trails, along the ridgeline adjacent to Lake Superior's North Shore from Duluth, Minnesota to the Canadian border. As of November 1992, the cutoff date for publication of this guide book, 185 of a projected 240 miles have been completed. With occasional small gaps, the Trail is completed from Two Harbors on the south-western end to the Canadian border on the northeastern end.

The Trail is the realization of an ambitious plan fostered by a group of visionaries – federal, state and local government employees, artists, resort and business owners, and hiking enthusiasts – who in 1986 incorporated the Superior Hiking Trail Association (SHTA) and made the first request for state funding for trail construction. Three grants from the Legislative Commission on Minnesota Resources (LCMR), each covering a two-year period (1987-89, 1989-91 and 1991-93), have been the principal source of funding for trail construction. The LCMR funds were used primarily to pay the salary of Tom Peterson, the trail construction coordinator "on loan" from the Minnesota Department of Natural Resources, to buy materials, and to finance the crews from the Minnesota Conservation Corps and Lake County that have built substantial portions of the Trail. Other important funding sources have included the U.S. Forest Service, Lake County, and private donations, including corporate contributions. 1993 marks the transition to new funding sources to complete the final portions of the Trail and to maintain that which is already built.

The Trail was officially opened with a ceremonial "log-cutting" in July 1987 at Britton Peak on the Sawbill Trail, an event attended by federal, state, and local officials and dignitaries, in addition to the Trail's founders. In August 1990, the SHTA sponsored a "Halfway Celebration" at Gooseberry Falls State Park, commemorating the completion of nearly 140 miles of trail – approximately halfway to the goal of a continuous footpath from Duluth to the Canadian border. This celebration was the culmination of the SHTA's first sponsored backpacking trip, in which a dozen hikers trekked the completed Trail in twelve rigorous days. They were greeted by another impressive contingent of dignitaries and well-wishers at Gooseberry Falls State Park.

In September 1991, the Trail was the site of the first "Superior 100" endurance run, in which long-distance "ultra-marathon" runners from around the country competed in a 100-mile race along the Trail. The race attracted more attention in 1992, and the sponsors plan to make it an annual event. The athletes participating in the event describe the Trail as one of the most challenging of the endurance run circuit. Comparing the "Superior 100" to other ultramarathon runs in the Sierras and Appalachians, Eric Clifton, winner of the 1992 run, described the Trail as "by far the prettiest 100 of all."

Though a relative newcomer to the country's long-distance trails, and a toddler by comparision with its prototype and model, the Appalachian Trail (conceived 70 years ago and completed, in its first layout, 15 years later), the Superior Hiking Trail has already won regional and even national recognition. It has been featured in count-less regional publications and broadcasts and has been the subject of stories in national magazines, such as *Prevention, Walking* and *Backpacker* magazines. *Prevention* identified the Superior Hiking Trail as one of the 12 best trails in the national forests.

— ANNE McKINSEY

General Description of the Trail

*T*he Superior Hiking Trail is designed as a footpath only, comprised principally of an 18-inch treadway through a clearing approximately four feet in width. SHTA policy prohibits the use of motorized vehicles, mountain bikes and horses on the Trail. The steepness and narrowness of the Trail in most areas make it unsuitable for cross-country skiing, although snowshoe travel is possible in many areas.

The Trail is routed principally along the ridgeline overlooking Lake Superior. At its lowest point, the Trail goes along the lakeshore, which is 602 feet above sea level. At its highest point, currently in the Sawtooth ridges northeast of the Cascade River, the Trail is 1750 feet above sea level and more than 1000 feet above Lake Superior. The Trail is characterized by ascents to rock outcroppings and cliffs, and descents into numerous river and creek valleys crossed by attractive and functional bridges. The Trail traverses a rich variety of terrain and habitat types. Woodlands of birch and aspen give way to stands of pine, fir and lush cedar groves. Grassy clearings, products of lumbering operations and forest fires, provide interesting variation from the more prevalent woodland scenes. Panoramic overlooks of Lake Superior, the Sawtooth Mountains and inland woodlands, lakes and rivers are abundant along the length of the Trail. At many points, the Trail follows rivers and creeks, often for distances of a mile or more, show-casing waterfalls and rapids, bends and deep gorges where thousands of years of rushing water has cut into layers of ancient volcanic bed-rock. Steep portions of the Trail are accessed by log and stone stair-ways handcrafted by trail crews.

Hikers enjoy varied forest scenes. The gradual transition from oak, maple and basswood to the boreal forest of balsam, pines, spruces, cedar and tamarack is interrupted by regrowth forest of aspen and birch. Wildlife abounds: encounters with deer are common, and sightings of moose, beaver, black bear, eagles and grouse. Fortunate hikers will remember many varieties of songbirds. Wildflowers are especially prevalent in the spring, but some varieties are evident through the hiking season. Wild blueberries and raspberries provide a special midsummer treat at many points along the Trail.

The Trail crosses national forest and state park lands, state and county property, and private property. Present plans intend that the Trail will reach the Canadian border near South Fowl Lake as well as through the Grand Portage Indian Reservation. The Trail will con-nect and traverse at least seven state parks. Many property owners – individuals and corporations, in addition to governmental units – have granted easements or permissions to cross their land for the construction of the Trail. In some areas, special restrictions apply as conditions of the permissions that have been granted on private lands. Please observe and obey all posted restrictions (such as requirements to stay on the Trail through private property, or prohibitions on fires, camping or hunting). The privilege to use these private lands depends upon the cooperation of Trail users and their respect for the special restrictions.

The one constant feature of the Trail, and the characteristic that distinguishes it from other forest trails, is the presence of Lake Supe-rior – the legendary lake Native Americans celebrated in song and story as "Gitche Gumme" (GI-chee GOO-me). Although the dis-tance to the big lake varies considerably along the Trail, its presence is always felt. Sometimes the "lake effect" weather brings cool breezes and moisture in to shore, though in summer it may be 20 degrees warmer just over the ridge. The Trail features many spectacular views of the Lake, as well as many more subtle views through the trees, allowing the hiker an endless selection of spots to rest, lunch and meditate against the backdrop of Lake Superior's many moods and colors. From some vantage points, the Wisconsin/Michigan shoreline is visible on the horizon; other views feature islands – Isle Royale on the northern part of the Trail, and the Apostles on the southern end.

Lake Superior itself is 31,280 square miles – the largest freshwater lake in the world by area. It is 350 miles long and 160 miles wide at its furthest dimensions. Its average depth is 489 feet, and its maximum depth is 1333 feet. As a part of the Great Lakes shipping corridor, it is the inland terminus of a commercial shipping trade that reaches to the East Coast and across the Atlantic Ocean. After the ice departs Duluth harbor in spring until sometime in December, the hiker can spot big vessels on the lake – the ore and grain freighters that carry midwestern exports to points east, and the "salties" that come from ports across the ocean. In the summer months when the lake is more often placid than angry, hikers can see sailboats, charter fishing boats and even small motorboats, canoes, and kayaks near the shore. The Lake's shipwrecks are legendary, and are documented at places such as the Split Rock Lighthouse visitor center and in books and paintings found in the many galleries and shops along the North Shore. Lake Superior, with its history and its beauty, gives the Superior Hiking Trail a unique and unforgettable character.

Accessing and using the trail

The Superior Hiking Trail is accessible directly from Minnesota Highway 61, on spur trails accessed from 61, or on many intersecting roads. Seven of the state parks along the North Shore (including Crosby-Manitou State Park, which is inland) are connected by the Superior Hiking Trail and provide access to it. Along Highway 61, look for the brown signs with the Superior Hiking Trail logo on them. The distance between access points – most from five to ten miles apart – makes the Trail easily divisible into one-way day-hikes, accomplished by leaving a vehicle at the access point destination and shuttling to the next access point to begin the hike. If your party does not have two vehicles, shuttles may be arranged through some of the local resorts or outfitters. Numerous other possibilities exist for day hikes and loop hikes, some employing state park or national forest trails. Of course, a hike to a point on the trail with a return along the same trail is never a disappointment. The vista you missed over your shoulder on the way in is revealed in all its splendor on the way out. Rewarding day-hikes are spotlighted in this book, including the "One-Car Hiker" on page 47.

When planning a hike, allow one hour for every one-and-a-half to three miles. Day-hikers should carry a pack with adequate water (river and lake water along the Trail must be treated before it is consumed), snacks, sunscreen, bug repellent, toilet paper, compass, flashlight, and an extra clothing layer and raingear if conditions warrant. Remember that weather conditions can change rapidly; dark storm clouds and chilly winds sometimes move in quickly and unexpectedly on what began as a warm, cloudless day. If you plan to hike more than one or two hours, it is best to be prepared for weather changes.

Each season of the year offers its own rewards for the Superior Hiking Trail hiker. Spring is a time for wildflowers, bird songs, and the unique color of emerging leaves. Summer brings the long hiking days and the sort of heat that makes a dip in one of the cool rivers all the more inviting. Fall is a symphony of colors and smells on the Trail, and the lack of biting insects makes it the friendliest time of year to hike. Fall also brings on deer hunting season. Hiking during hunting season obviously causes special risks. The best advice would probably be to confine your hiking to state parks where hunting is prohibited. Regardless of where you hike, however, be sure to wear blaze orange clothing and stay alert.

The Trail is also ideally suited for long-distance hiking. The hiker seeking an extended trip can hike the 200 miles of the Superior Hiking Trail to its eastern end, then continue along the Border Route Trail, which in turn links with the Kekekabic Trail. These connections provide a multi-week adventure of over 300 miles, from near Ely in the west to near Grand Portage in the east, and thence southwestward to Two Harbors on the Superior Hiking Trail.

For additional information about backpacking on the Trail and tips for overnight trips, see the chapter on backpacking on the Trail.

For the long-distance hiker who prefers more amenities, lodge-to-lodge hiking is available. You need only carry a daypack, since luggage is transported to your destination each day. For more information on lodge-to-lodge hiking, contact the Lutsen-Tofte Tourism Association at (218) 663-7804, or toll-free at (800) 622-4019, ext. 730.

This guidebook is designed to be a functional resource for you to plan your hiking adventure on the Superior Hiking Trail. The body of text is broken into segments, with a description of each Trail section, and information on parking, access points and campsites. In addition, the highlights of each segment are featured – rivers, waterfalls, overlooks and other natural features. To enhance your hiking experience, information on human and natural history, both fact and legend, are also included, as well as explanations for some of the natural phenomena observed. At selected overlooks, the book tells you what you are seeing in the distance. Often when the Superior Hiking Trail intersects state park and other trails, maps of those areas are provided to help you plan loop hikes. This information will maximize your enjoyment of the Trail.

— ANNE McKINSEY

GENERAL DESCRIPTION OF TRAIL

Geology and Scenery along the North Shore

$\mathcal{M}$innesota's shorelands of Lake Superior — the "North Shore" — is a land of rugged, forested hills, sweeping vistas of blue, green, autumn red and gold, and winter white, rocky headlands and crashing waves, cozy valleys and surging waterfalls. The dramatically beautiful landscape that we see today is a consequence of a geological history that goes back more than a billion years, into Late Precambrian time.

Regional geologic studies have shown that what is now the upper Great Lakes area had undergone several major periods of volcanism, intense deformation of the Earth's crust, sedimentation and mountain-building. By about 1200 million years ago, erosion had eventually reduced the area to a low, rolling plain. There were no Great Lakes.

Then about 1100 million years ago the center of North America began to split apart as slow upwellings in the Earth's stiff-plastic mantle (beneath the crust) began to melt, and huge volumes of molten rock (magma) leaked up to the surface along fissures in the crust. The present remains of this world-scale crustal feature, known as the Mid-Continent Rift System, extend from southeastern Michigan north through the lower peninsula, westward through Lake Superior, and south-southwest beneath the Twin Cities and Iowa to northeast Kansas. Most of the magma was erupted as great, pancake-like flows of "flood basalt," of a composition similar to the modern or recent eruptions on Hawaii, Iceland or the Snake River Plain in Idaho. Hundreds of individual lava flows erupted, building up a sequence of layers up to 5 miles thick along the North Shore area and even thicker along the axis of the rift, now under the Lake.

As the crust was pulled apart, stretched and thinned, and magma erupted onto the surface from the mantle beneath, the center of the rift gradually subsided, leaving the rock layers tilted on the flanks towards the rift axis. Erosion during the last billion years has etched out these tilted layers to form the "Sawtooth Mountains" in Cook County. These are a series of long ridges with a relatively gentle southeast slope toward Lake Superior and a steep northwest slope, each one sculpted from a single huge lava flow.

Some basaltic magma never made it to the surface, but squeezed between older layers and solidified at various levels in the crust. When magma cools and crystallizes slowly it tends to produce larger crystals and the rocks thus formed (intrusive rocks) are generally more resistant when eventually exposed to erosion at the Earth's surface. A very large complex of intrusions, the Duluth Complex, underlies prominent highlands stretching from downtown Duluth southwestward past Spirit Mountain to Bardon Peak, and overlooks the St. Louis River valley and Wisconsin. (This same Duluth Complex also extends inland northward almost to Ely and eastward into Cook County).

Smaller intrusions, mainly the dark rock diabase, squeezed in at higher levels within the lava-flow sequence. Some of these make up such prominent hills along the North Shore as Hawk Ridge at Duluth, Silver Cliff, most of the rugged highlands between Beaver Bay and Little Marais, Leveaux and Oberg Mountains and the ski hills at Lutsen. Diabase hills continue in the Hovland area beyond Grand Portage, with the great ramparts of Hat Point, Mt. Josephine and the ridge beyond that overlooks Wauswaugoning Bay.

In some places these diabase magmas carried up huge blocks of a whitish rock called anorthosite, torn loose from the base of the crust about 25 miles beneath the surface. These anorthosites are very resistant to erosion, and now "hold up" such landmarks as Split Rock Lighthouse, Mt. Trudee and other knobs in Tettegouche State Park, and the greatest of all, Carlton Peak at Tofte.

The great volumes of hot magma that worked their way up through the older crust melted some of it. This new magma had the composition of rhyolite or granite, with more silica and less iron than the basaltic magmas, and when it solidified it formed light-colored rocks in contrast to the dark basalt and diabase. Several very large rhyolite flows erupted; one of them forms the magnificent features of Palisade Head and Shovel Point in Lake County. Big rhyolites have also been eroded to form the deep gorges of the Devil Track, Kadunce, and Brule Rivers in Cook County, and of Split Rock River in Lake County.

For some as yet unknown reason, rifting and volcanism ended fairly abruptly without the continent coming completely apart to form a new ocean basin. The last major volcanic sequence can now be seen as the "backbone" of Isle Royale and of Keweenaw Point, far across the Lake in Michigan. The rift continued to sink for awhile, however, and streams washed sand, pebbles and mud into the slowly subsiding basin. Several miles of such sediment accumulated in the middle, some of which can be seen today on the Bayfield Peninsula and Apostle Islands, Wisconsin. Finally, over a period of perhaps 100 million years, the crust stabilized, and the buried sediments gradually hardened into rock. The most dramatic episode in Lake Superior history was over, and erosion by streams took over. But there was still no Lake Superior.

The last chapter in the saga of the North Shore's landscape is the Great Ice Age. Several times during the last two million years (most recently only about 14,000 years ago) great continental glaciers, up to one or two miles thick, built up and oozed southward from Canada.

The great ice streams were mainly eroding the underlying rock, some of which had become deeply weathered. Moving southwestward, the Superior Lobe of the ice sheet carried debris (including volcanic rocks, agates and sandstone) from the North Shore area as far as the Twin Cities, the Minnesota River Valley, and even to Iowa. The ice found the sedimentary rocks in the middle of the old Midcontinent Rift System to be relatively easy to erode, and it excavated what was to be the Lake Superior basin well below sea level. As the glacier melted back about 11,000 years ago, it uncovered this great scooped-out depression which of course filled with water. Early stages (such as Glacial Lake Duluth) were several hundred feet higher than the present Lake, because the ice was still blocking the outlet. Look for rounded beach stones along the Trail, high above the current Lake level. About 5000 years ago, Lake Superior as we know it today was well established. Since glaciation the forests have covered the land, the North Shore rivers have been eroding their gorges, and waves have been making beaches and eating away at the shore cliffs and bluffs.

As you hike the trail, remember this geologic history that has shaped the landscape. Look for evidence of volcanic activity, the "squeezed in" intrusions, glacial erosion and deposition, abandoned beaches far above the present Lake level and on-going geologic processes. Enjoy the Geologic Dimension!

— JOHN GREEN

GEOLOGY AND SCENERY

Trees and Plants
of the Superior Hiking Trail

The Superior Hiking Trail follows a corridor that is long enough to have members of three general vegetational groups along its length. One of these is hardwood forest that is at the northwestern limit of its distribution. These northern hardwoods, such as maple and oak, are concentrated in the highlands that form the setting for so much of the Trail. This group become less common as one travels northeastward from Duluth, and some species disappear completely by Cook County. The second group includes boreal species ranging across northern Minnesota. As the northern hardwoods thin out to the northeast, this second group becomes more prevalent along the Trail. The third group consists of species found primarily to the east along the U.S./Canada border but not ranging far to the north or south. The eastern white pine is typical of the border group.

Members from each of these forest "groups" exist side-by-side in a wide variety of different plant communities. By understanding where a tree comes from geographically, you can begin to make sense of why it is found in particular parts of the Trail. For example, you will find white spruce often in dark, cool valleys which better resemble northern habitat than the warmer, drier ridgetops. Glaciers deposited the rare deep soil along some of the ridges, providing a soil and a habitat for maples quite similar to that found in states further to the south.

The northern hardwood group

Sugar maple is typically the most common tree in the northern hardwoods. Like many others in this group, it is associated with upper slopes, which are less frosty in the late spring. Sugar maple stands occur in all segments of the Trail. They were tapped for sugar by the Ojibway people. Sugar maple forests make fall hikes on the Trail glorious, turning hillsides into gold and red. Sugar maples can be identified by their leaves, whose well-known shape is seen on the Canadian flag.

Northern red oak is another northern hardwood. It is a large tree at the southwest end of the Trail. However, at the end of its range near the Lake/Cook County line, oaks are a small tree on rocky knobs. Its deep maroon leaves are among the last to drop in the fall.

Yellow birch can grow to the greatest diameter of any of the northern hardwoods. It may be identified in all seasons by scraping the bark from a twig and sniffing for the distinctive odor of wintergreen. These trees sometimes begin life on a dead log, which later rots away to leave a yellow birch growing "on stilts." This species often develops a hollow trunk, and so is an important site for animal denning or nesting.

Other, less common members of this group include basswood, ironwood (hop hornbeam) and American elm.

The boreal forest group

Paper birch is extremely common throughout all but wet ground along the Trail. Its white bark and black twigs are more distinctive than its rather plain leaves. This tree requires sunny conditions for growth and fades from the scene as forest stands age and shade the forest floor. Droughts in the late 1980's have led to an extensive dieback of this species, especially near roads and clearcuts.

Balsam fir is a common tree in all parts of the Trail corridor. It seldom achieves great age or size before a storm knocks it down or spruce budworm kills it. Its needles are "flat and friendly," which distinguishes it from the "spiky" spruce. Crushing these needles will bring out an aroma reminiscent of winter holidays.

White spruce thrives throughout the Trail corridor where soils are deep enough. You can roll its needles between two fingers, and its bark is rougher than the balsam fir's bark. Large individuals are found here and there. On rock outcrops or in bogs, you may see black spruce, a smaller species. Black spruce is otherwise uncommon because of the scarcity of bogs near Lake Superior.

White cedar is common on both wet streams and dry rock outcrops, but only occasional on deep, well-drained soils. What these seemingly contradictory habitats have in common is a lower frequency of fire. White cedar, wherever you find it, is an important winter food for deer. You can identify this tree by its broad, flat, scaly needles and its stringy bark.

Balsam poplar is found predominantly in wet soil near streams. The long, sticky aromatic buds are distinctive, and perfume the woods during leaf out in the spring.

Mountain maple is a small tree or shrub with multiple stems. It grows in the understory of many kinds of trees on the uplands.

Jack pine is scarce along the North Shore in general. The damp summer and lack of expanses of coarse or shallow soils curtail the frequency of the fires on which this species depends.

The border group

Several species have their ranges centered in the U.S./Canada border region to the east of Lake Superior. They overlap about equally with the northern portion of the hardwoods and the southern portion of the boreal forest.

Among these species is white pine. White pine is a distinctively majestic tree, with its feathery branches and dark trunk. On closer examination, you'll find that the needles come in clumps of five, as opposed to clumps of two with the red pine. This species was abundant over much of the North Shore region prior to logging. If you see a large, rotting stump on your hike, it is likely the remnant of a white pine that fell to the lumberjacks. The North Shore has a climate that is extremely favorable for the white pine blister rust fungus, so efforts to replant this species have been less successful here than in many other former pineries.

Red pine grows in scattered groves, often associated with rock outcrops. Like white pine, it was more abundant before the logging era, though not as common as its five-needled cousin. Disease does not currently pose a great threat to this species, which is also known as "Norway Pine" and is the state tree of Minnesota.

Black ash is found mostly in damp ground, rarely with hardwoods on the uplands. It is abundant near many streams. This species seems to be the ultimate in caution, as it is the last to leaf out and the first to drop its leaves.

Heartleaf birch is a little-known tree that barely enters the North Shore from the east. It resembles paper birch, but has a rosy tinge to its bark. Also, it tends to have branches farther down the trunk than does paper birch, as heartleaf birch is more tolerant of shade. Despite the name, leaf shape is not easy to use for identification. In fact, some botanists list this as a variety of paper birch. This is the only tree species that is added as one proceeds northeastward on the Trail. Look for it in Cook and eastern Lake Counties.

Trembling aspen, also known as "popple" or "poplar," fits into none of the above groups, and yet is one of the most common trees on the Trail. This species occupies more territory than any other North American tree, being found well to the north, south, east and west (with a hiatus in the Great Plains). It can be expected in the

Trail corridor wherever there are younger forests on deep soils. Old, shady stands are unlikely to have much aspen, although large trembling aspen are found in some places. This species increased greatly as the land was opened up by lumbering for pine and by the fires that sometimes followed.

This diversity of tree types parallels a diversity of wildflowers and other herbaceous growth. Minor variations in soil types can lead to major changes in the flora on the forest floor. Some stretches of rich soil will be covered with large-leaf aster and bluebead lily, while bare granitic rock may support some caribou moss and the polypody fern. Each month of spring, summer, and fall brings a new range of color and growth. As the snow melts in spring, look for violets, marsh marigold and wild lily-of-the-valley. As summer nears, the moccasin flowers and ladyslippers bloom, often in isolated and hard-to-find patches. In the heat of summer, watch for columbine, wild roses, buttercup and the towering cow parsnip. The onset of fall brings the asters and the goldenrods, which can bloom well into October.

Other flowers grow in distinct habitats, such as the water lilies and cattails in marshes, labrador tea and bog laurel in bogs, and twinflower, wintergreen and indian pipe in pine duff.

Overall, let these clues of trees and flowers guide you to an understanding of the varied terrain through which the Trail passes. On any given section of the Trail you will pass through three, four, or a dozen different habitats. Landforms, microclimates and succession determined these habitats, and the trees and other plants tell you fascinating stories about survival, and thriving, in the North Woods.

—CINDY JOHNSON-GROH & ANDREW SLADE

Birds of the Lake Superior Highlands

One of the great pleasures in walking through the woods is being attuned to what other creatures are inhabiting the same piece of ground. Most forest animals are wary (at least those higher taxonomically than insects!), and their presence is not easily revealed. Birds, because they fly and they sing while nesting, are more conspicuous than most other vertebrates and thus add a dimension to the hike, whether you are teasing out a scolding ovenbird from the undergrowth or watching hawks migrate in the fall from one of the many overlooks.

The type of birdwatching you may experience along the Superior Hiking Trail depends on the character of the woods, the season of the year and the weather. Dedicated bird-watchers with a penchant for listing notable species travel to the North Shore in search of gulls, sea ducks, and out-of-range migrants accidently appearing on the shore of Lake Superior. This search can be exciting sport, but an equally rewarding experience can be found in discovering what birds inhabit the forest that covers the hills back from shore. Now that the Trail provides good access to these woods, one can hike, look and listen for some of the approximately 100 species of birds that breed in the Lake

Superior Highlands in summer. During both spring and fall migration, congregations of woodland birds are occasionally encountered, but the winter woods are virtually silent since most of the birds have gone to more southerly wintering grounds.

Lake Superior Highlands describes the ecoregion that the Superior Hiking Trail traverses. Ecoregions are defined by topography, climate, soils and vegetation. Habitat for birds is almost entirely determined by the vegetation, which on the forested hills of the Lake Superior Highlands is a mixture of deciduous and coniferous types with hardwood forest types predominant. Openings, either woodland ponds and streams, brushlands or cutovers, provide variety as does an occasional boreal conifer bog or open ledge.

These unusual habitats provide opportunities to see some rare nesting species.

Four species of raptors (turkey vulture, osprey, bald eagle, peregrine falcon) might be spotted flying over the forest from a rocky knob or pond edge. Two other species, red-tailed hawk and American kestrel, could be encountered nesting in forest that has been broken up by logging or other clearings. The deep-woods hawks, sharp-shinned, goshawk and broad-winged, are more numerous but rarely seen. The best evidence of their presence is the alarm cries

Birds of ponds and streams

wood duck
common goldeneye
hooded merganser
mallard
blue-winged teal
ring-necked duck
great blue heron
tree swallow
spotted sandpiper
kingfisher

Rare breeding birds

olive-sided flycatcher
yellow-bellied flycatcher
gray jay
boreal chickadee
Connecticut warbler
Lincoln's sparrow

given near a nesting site. Merlins are also very vociferous near the nest but are mostly found around big conifers along lakeshores.

Woodland ponds provide a place to see ducks, especially those that nest in tree cavities. A small colony of great blue herons or tree swallows might be discovered in a beaver pond and spotted sandpipers can be found bobbing along the rocks of open streams.

Where boreal conifer lowlands intersect the upland forest, a number of species confined to that special habitat can be located. Some of them, because they are rare breeders on a national scale, are much sought after by birders. Pockets of shrubby wetlands or water edges provide habitat for another group of species not otherwise present in the forested hills.

The greatest portion of the species present along the Superior Hiking Trail, about three-fourths, are upland forest inhabitants, most of whom are only there for a short period of time during the breeding season (early May to early August). At least 73 species probably nest in these uplands, including the three hawks mentioned before, four owls (great horned, barred, long-eared, saw-whet), five other non-passerines (ruffed grouse, black-billed cuckoo, whip-poor-will, chimney swift, ruby-throated hummingbird), five woodpeckers and 56 passerines (songbirds).

A very few of these birds are permanent residents and might be found in winter woods on a snowshoe trek. The rest are here in the summer to take advantage of the abundant insects (mostly caterpillars) to feed their young, and the many diverse habitats provided by the mixed forest, including its cut-over patches and natural shrubby openings.

The diversity of the upland forest is the key to the richness of nesting species found there. Although most of the contiguous forest is deciduous, it is mixed with varying amounts of conifers which sometimes form fairly pure stands. The age of the forest also varies from young, shrubby stands to big, old trees that form a dense canopy.

Each habitat type has certain species that are adapted to what it provides for food and shelter, but some species are more specialized in their requirements than others. Those that are mostly restricted to wetlands and openings have already been mentioned and since these habitats are rare along the Trail, so are these species.

There are 73 species that are considered upland, forest-dependent breeding birds. The raptors (hawks and owls) have already been listed. They have large territories and their population density is quite small, so spotting one is a thrill. Most of the other forest nesting birds are more abundant, but small songbirds are not easily noticed in the thick vegetation. About half of the woodland birds belong to just four taxonomic families: thrushes (5 species), vireos (4 species), warblers (17 species) and sparrows/finches (11 species).

The summer hiker who is not a birder is probably amazed that the woods contain so many species. Except for the dawn chorus (starting from 4:30 a.m. when even a dedicated nature explorer is likely asleep) their presence is only revealed by scolding chips or an occasional burst of song. To really appreciate the birds along the Trail, learning the songs, at least of some of the common species, adds immense pleasure to the hiking experience. The intense singing

Birds of shrubby wetlands

American woodcock
alder flycatcher
gray catbird
golden-winged warbler*
Tennessee warbler*
northern waterthrush
common yellowthroat
Wilson's warbler*
swamp sparrow
*rare

Permanent residents

goshawk
great horned owl
barred owl
downy woodpecker
hairy woodpecker
pileated woodpecker
blue jay
common raven
black-capped chickadee
red-breasted nuthatch
pine siskin
evening grosbeak

period is at the height of the nesting cycle which is a very short time from early June to early July. There are some good, commercial birding tapes that aid in learning bird songs, but the best way is spotting the songster with binoculars and identifying it while it sings.

Two species are much prized by birders because the North Shore forest is the only place in Minnesota that they are known to regularly breed: Philadelphia vireo and black-throated blue warbler.

Weather is always a variable in bird-watching and windy days slow down song and other bird activity considerably. However, in the fall it is on those glorious days with a good northwest wind, following the passage of a cold front, that hawk-watching is the most rewarding. Hawks, and other day-time migrants, are funneled along the shore of Lake Superior and use the updrafts from the hills to aid them in their flight. The bulk of the hawk migration is from about the 10th of September through the 10th of October, but eagles and northern raptors can be seen on days with good migration weather through early December.

The overlooks along the Trail provide opportunities for witnessing this migration although concentrations are not nearly as large as near Duluth. Other birds migrate in flocks, usually in the morning, and can be seen in numbers in a wide band along the North Shore in the fall: blue jay, American crow, common raven, American robin, cedar waxwing and seven species of winter finches.

Both spring (May) and fall (September through early October), flocks of small birds can be encountered, usually spotted feeding intensely in the treetops (vireos and warblers) or flushed while walking along the Trail (thrushes and sparrows). Their presence depends on the weather they have encountered during migration. Local breeding birds also congregate in foraging flocks after the nesting season and before they set out on their long-distance migration to the tropics. They are often joined by the permanent residents, chickadees and woodpeckers, who usually announce their presence by their flocking calls.

Each hiking trip, depending on time and place, can produce a different experience with the birds in the woods. Storing up these moments expands the memory of the event and can also add to the knowledge of the birds of the Lake Superior Highlands.

— JANET C. GREEN

**The 17
most common
upland birds**

*least flycatcher
veery*
American robin*
red-eyed vireo*
Nashville warbler
chestnut-sided warbler*
magnolia warbler
black-throated green warbler
blackburnian warbler
black-and-white warbler
American redstart
ovenbird*
mourning warbler
Canada warbler
rose-breasted grosbeak
song sparrow
white-throated sparrow**

*especially abundant

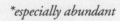

Animals of the
Superior Hiking Trail

Describing the animal life of the North Shore and the Superior Hiking Trail is a little like serving a good pan of lasagna – no matter how you slice it up, there's never enough to satisfy everyone. Fortunately, for the sake of brevity it's possible to make some distinctions. First of all, there are animals in the official sense, that is, things which move and eat other things. But then there are "animals," generally fuzzy things with one set of eyes. Is that black fly biting your earlobe an animal? Yes, indeed. But a lot of people would rather swat the black fly while looking for "real" animals like a deer, wolf or turtle. Insects, reptiles, fish, and amphibians are all animals but, due to space, will receive only short notice here. And the birds of the Superior Hiking Trail are covered in the previous chapter. This chapter will mostly cover the mammals of the Superior Hiking Trail.

As you hike, you may encounter animals of three basic types:

1) Small animals which are common but seldom seen.

2) Medium-size animals which are somewhat common and often seen.

3) Medium-to-large, generally carnivorous animals which are rare, wide-ranging and also seldom seen.

On your typical day hike you probably won't see a lot of animals besides birds and insects. That's not because they aren't there. But unless you have the eyes of a hawk, you'll likely miss the mice and shrews that cruise the underbrush. And unless you are quiet and lucky, you probably won't see a wolf. However, white-tail deer, the snowshoe hare and the red squirrel, among others, are animals which are commonly seen along the Superior Hiking Trail.

Although you may not see any large mammal, you will undoubtedly see some evidence of their passing. They are out there. Many mammals are active during the morning and evenings, but rest during the day. The white-tail deer you see bounding through the forest may have been resting from a busy night of feeding before you startled it. If you want to learn about the animals of the Superior Hiking Trail, you will do better to look for evidence rather than the animal itself.

If you do look for animal signs, you won't be disappointed. In a muddy section of the Trail, look for tracks of deer, moose and wolves, animals likely to use the Superior Hiking Trail as an easy path through remote woods. Scat (animal feces) is another obvious sign, and becomes more obvious when an animal uses scat to mark territory. When there is a prominent, bare rock near the Trail, look for wolf or coyote scat (told by the ropy texture, hair and bone chip content) or that of the fisher or marten (which is long, slender, and dark). All these mammals use scat to mark their territory, with both its sight and smell. Other signs of large animals include bark rubbings by male moose and deer, deer and moose beds in grassy areas, and nests. If this sort of animal watching interests you, bring a field guide such as Peterson's guide to animal tracks. There are some fascinating stories to be read in the woods.

Small animals which are common but seldom seen

This category includes all the shrews, voles, mice and little weasels. These animals are used to fleeing at the sound (or feel) of danger. You'll see their trails crossing above or sometimes below the Trail. In open areas, look for the birds like kestrels who are looking, in turn, for these little creatures. At dusk in a campsite a woodland deer mouse or short-tailed shrew might try to get into your food or clean up your dinner scraps.

These small creatures play important roles in ecosystems, as primary consumers and carnivores (mostly of insects). They also aerate and enrich the soil with their tunnels. For every one large, dramatic carnivore in the food web there are thousands of little creatures, all doing their part to keep the cycles flowing. And in case you are fortunate enough to encounter one, remember that the short-tailed shrew is one of only two North American mammals with a venomous bite.

Medium-to-large size animals which are somewhat common and often seen

• White-tail deer

Although the deer is a common resident now, a century ago there were hardly any here. Instead there were woodland caribou, which thrived on lichens and moss of the primordial forest. Now, with logging and other habitat changes, the caribou are only in Canada (with the notable exception of a caribou wandering in Hovland in the winter of 1980-81). Deer congregate along the North Shore in winter and early spring, where snowfall is lighter and melts sooner, making food more accessible and travel easier. The Jonvik deer yard near Lutsen is one of the largest deer yards in the state. For two weeks in the fall, generally the first and second weeks in November, deer are hunted all along the Superior Hiking Trail, except in state parks, so wear bright colors.

• *Moose*

Count yourself fortunate if you encounter one of these gentle giants on your hike. You'll increase your luck if you look carefully in the low, wet areas near the Trail. Look for a brown boulder moving among the lily pads. In general, deer and moose populations do not intermix. The deer carry a flatworm which doesn't harm the deer but is fatal to the moose. Moose droppings are thumb-size, light brown pellets, found in large piles. Moose tracks have the same double half-moon shape of the deer, but are at least twice as long. Some classic moose habitat along the Superior Hiking Trail includes Jonvik Creek and the wetlands around Grand Portage.

• *Black bear*

The black bear is an incredible survivor. It uses every trick in the book to survive the North Woods. Bears have one of the most diverse natural diets around, including your food bag, if you're not careful. Bears' diet follows the season: when the blueberries are ripe, they gorge on blueberries, and likewise with the hazelnuts or other edibles. When there's no more fresh food, around the end of September, bears begin to go into torpor, a sort of intermittant hibernation. The Superior Hiking Trail passes near a grove of oak trees in Tettegouche State Park which is a magnet for bears from fifty miles around when the acorns are ripe in the fall. Treat these creatures with the respect they deserve – that includes putting your food far out of reach when you're camping.

• *Weasels*

You may not see a weasel, but weasels are mammals worth noting. There is a whole family of weasels of all different sizes, all with the same mode of survival: chase and kill. The short-tailed weasel, or ermine, chases mice; the fisher and marten chase larger prey such as squirrels and hares. You'll be thrilled if you ever witness one of their chases. In the winter, look for their distinctive bounding tracks in the snow.

• *Snowshoe hare*

Depending on their population cycles, you may see lots of hares or you may see none. Even if they are around, you have to look carefully. With their changing coat, they are always well camouflaged. They prefer thickets of shrubs and short trees, which give them plenty of cover from predators such as great-horned owls and lynx.

• *Red squirrel*

The sound of a red squirrel defending its territory is one of the standard anthems of the North Woods. That sharp, rattling *chirrrr* is the squirrel's way of telling you to beat it. Each squirrel defends a territory of about a 200 yard diameter circle. If the summer and fall harvests are good, the squirrel will store up to 14,000 food items in this territory, including cones, mushrooms and nuts (the mushrooms are hung on tree bark where they can dry). Red squirrels can become overly friendly in campsites if they are fed by hikers.

• *Beaver*

As the Trail works its way up and down hills and across streams, it is bound to take you through the work of the beaver. Sometimes, though, you won't even notice. The beaver, with its propensity to change the environment to suit its needs (like another mammal, *Homo Sapiens*), has been around long enough that its ponds have turned into forests. Some particularly spectacular beaver ponds can be found near the Arrowhead Trail and on Jonvik Creek, where the Trail crosses the creek on a beaver dam (or, if the canoe is on your side, by the boat), as well as along the upper reaches of the Gooseberry River.

Medium-to-large, generally carnivorous animals which are rare, wide-ranging and also seldom seen

• **Timber wolf**

Along the North Shore, starting northeast of Two Harbors, there are numerous packs of wolves. This is, however, the fringe of their population. The traffic and development of Highway 61 keeps most wolves inland, though the Superior Hiking Trail leads through some prime wolf territory. To see a wolf you would have to know their travel paths and disguise yourself from sight or smell. Look for scat and tracks along the Trail, also the occasional kill site of a well-broken-up deer carcass. The presence of the wolves is a testimony to the wildness of the land through which you are travelling.

• **Coyote**

Where there aren't wolves along the North Shore, there are likely to be coyotes. Wolves defend their territories from coyotes, but as the edge of wolf range fluctuates, so does the coyote range. Coyotes are smaller than wolves but larger than foxes, and can be identified by their large ears and bouncing gait. They're more of a "suburban" animal, more accustomed to human presence. Like wolves, they have eerie, though distinct howling sessions.

• **Lynx and Bobcat**

Solitary hunters, these wild cats prey mostly on the snowshoe hare, and so their populations vary with the hare's. The bobcat is at the northern edge of its range and the lynx is at its southern edge. The lynx travels 3-6 miles a night in search of food, but success is less than 50/50 each night. Both cats have ranges rather than territories, which means they can overlap with others of the same species and are not generally defended. Another even bigger cat, the mountain lion, has been spotted in recent years in St. Louis and Cook Counties.

Other animals on the Superior Hiking Trail

Insects are animals, right? If you're out in May through September, you'll likely encounter some of these. Not all of them are out to bite you, either. But some will try. Watch for black flies in May and June, various species of mosquito from May to September, and deer and horse flies in July and August. Look for dragonflies, leeches, colorful beetles, and aquatic insects in the streams. Also in the streams you'll find brook trout, and a host of frogs, turtles, and salamanders.

The animal life along the North Shore is a significant part of what makes the Trail so special. With careful observation, you'll find that there is a world of creatures as wild and dramatic as the cliffs and mountains of the Shore. As you wind your way through different habitats, keep an eye out for the "locals." Either a sighting or a sign will let you in on part of the great mystery of this land.

— ANDREW SLADE

ANIMALS

General North Shore History

The first people to enter the North Shore region arrived around 10,000 years ago. These Native Americans, called Paleo-Indians, entered the region during the final retreat of the Wisconsin Glaciation. As the Superior ice lobe melted back to the northeast it blocked the present outlet of Lake Superior causing lake levels to rise above their present level by up to 450 feet.

This enlarged Lake Superior is known as Glacial Lake Duluth, and in many areas the ancient shoreline closely follows the ridgeline which much of the Superior Hiking Trail now follows. The Paleo-Indians were big game hunters of caribou, bison, musk ox and possibly mammoth. In all probability, these hunters followed the shoreline of this lake of glacial meltwater along these present-day ridge tops.

The Old Copper Culture followed the Paleo-Indian cultural tradition around Lake Superior and existed from about 5000 years ago until about 2000 years ago. During this time the Indians used raw native copper, found on Isle Royale and in northern Michigan, hammering it into tools. Occasionally copper artifacts, in the form of spear points, knives, and fish hooks, are found along the North Shore. (If you find copper or stone tools contact the state archaeologist in

Duluth at (218) 726-7154. These finds are very rare and the information will add to the knowledge of this early history.)

Many waves of Indian people inhabited the North Shore prior to European contact. The first Europeans, French explorers and fur traders, first reached the Lake Superior country about 1620. At that time, the Ojibway (also called Anishinabe or Chippewa) inhabited the eastern end of the lake as far west as the Upper Peninsula of Michigan. Their culture centered at the rapids at the outlet of the big lake. By 1650 the French had encountered the Dakota, or Sioux, at the head of the lake. Along the North Shore lived the Assiniboine and the Cree. As the fur trade moved west over the next one hundred years, so did the Ojibway, displacing by 1750 the Dakota, the Assiniboine, and the Cree, who removed farther to the west and north.

By 1780, the Europeans had established fur trading posts at the mouth of the St. Louis River and at Grand Portage. The Ojibway were firmly established on the western end of the lake and in northeastern Minnesota. Both Europeans and Ojibway navigated their frail birch bark canoes along the rugged North Shore between these two important sites of early commerce and, although the Ojibway did have foot trails heading inland at different points along the shore, the early traders had little reason to leave the lake and explore the adjacent uplands.

In 1854, the Ojibway signed the Treaty of La Pointe which opened up northeastern Minnesota to mineral exploration and settlement. The first permanent settlement was a group of Germans from Ohio who settled at Beaver Bay in 1856. The late 1800's saw a rise of commercial herring fishing along the North Shore, and it was said that nearly every cove harbored at least one fisherman's shanty.

Across Lake Superior, Michigan lumber barons had cut most of the big stands of virgin white pine in Michigan by 1890. They then set their sights on Lake Superior's North Shore. Between 1890 and 1910, millions of board feet of red and white pine were cut from the hills along the North Shore. Temporary railroads transported the logs down to the Lake where they were rafted up and towed by tugboat to sawmills in Duluth, Superior, Bayfield and Ashland. Today many of these old railroad grades – most used only for one or two seasons – are still visible. In places, the Superior Hiking Trail either crosses or follows some of these straight and level grades such as the Alger, Nestor and Merrill-Ring grades.

Ever since northeastern Minnesota was opened to exploration, mining has had an active history on the North Shore. Small, unproductive copper explorations began along some of the rivers in the 1850's and 1860's. In 1884, high-grade iron ore from the Iron Ranges in northeastern Minnesota started shipping from the huge ore docks in Two Harbors on ore boats bound for the mills on the lower lakes.

At the turn of the century a new company was formed in Two Harbors, Minnesota Mining and Manufacturing. Known today as 3M, the company planned to mine an abrasive rock, believed to be Carborundum, at Crystal Bay near the mouth of the Baptism River. At the same time the North Shore Abrasives Company was formed to mine the same type of rock from a location near Split Rock. In both cases the rock was found to be too soft to serve as an abrasive and mining operations were discontinued by 1906.

Taconite, a material refined from low-grade iron ore, was produced in the 1950's from mines on the Minnesota Iron Range. Taconite pellets continue to be processed and shipped to refineries on the lower Great Lakes from Duluth, Two Harbors, Silver Bay and Taconite Harbor. Operational railroad tracks crossed by the Superior Hiking Trail connect the mines near Ely, Babbitt and Hoyt Lakes with these shipping points along the North Shore.

It is obvious to anyone visiting the North Shore that tourism and recreation have had, and continue to have, a major impact on local development. As early as 1910, when Split Rock Lighthouse was built, the lightkeeper recorded that tourists began visiting the light station by sailboat. Even though a one-lane wagon road was built between certain points along the shore in the 1890's, the present North Shore highway was not completed between Duluth and the Canadian border until 1924. When the highway was completed, camping and cabin resorts sprang up along the shore. Seven state parks were set aside and protected, joined most recently by the eighth, Grand Portage State Park. Today, hikers on the Superior Hiking Trail can still look upon many of the same unspoiled vistas that the Native Americans and the first French explorers saw.

For more information on the cultures and peoples that have inhabited the North Shore, visit the Cook County Historical Society, the Lake County Historical Society, or the Split Rock Lighthouse visitor center.

— LEE RADZAK

About the
Superior Hiking Trail Association

*T*he *Superior Hiking Trail Association (SHTA) is a Minnesota* non-profit corporation whose members are dedicated to the completion, preservation and promotion of the Superior Hiking Trail. The original members of the SHTA were the visionaries – federal and state government representatives and local North Shore resort and business owners - who incorporated the SHTA and obtained the first funding to see their vision become a reality. From this small group, membership has grown to approximately 1350 in 1992, including members in 26 states and Canada.

The SHTA has one paid staff member working in a home office in Two Harbors. Apart from some work performed on contract, the remainder of the work of the SHTA is done by volunteers. A board of directors consisting of members from a variety of locations, careers, avocations, and age groups meets bi-monthly on the North Shore to make policy decisions for the SHTA. Committees of SHTA members are responsible for the substantive work of the Association, including trail maintenance, product sales, planning organized hikes, and preparation of the *Ridgeline* newsletter and other publications.

The most visible activities of the SHTA are the popular organized hikes scheduled throughout the hiking season, including wintertime snowshoe hikes. Hosted by SHTA members and featuring leaders with interpretive skills, such as naturalists, geologists, photographers, and historians, most of the SHTA-sponsored events are one-way day hikes with shuttle service allowing hikers to leave their cars at the final destination and hike to them at their own pace. The SHTA's hiking program also features backpacking trips of several days' duration. SHTA members also have the opportunity to attend the annual business meeting, scheduled in May, and to participate in a weekend full of hiking, fun, and comaraderie planned around the meeting.

Most of the trail was built by crews hired from the local communities and from the Minnesota Conservation Corps (MCC). MCC crews will likely continue to help maintain the Trail. Much additional maintenance is provided through a system of volunteers: some have taken responsibility for the upkeep of particular sections, others participate in scheduled maintenance hikes. Scout troops, outdoors clubs, and other organizations have undertaken trail maintenance responsibilities. Individual hikers and groups can give something back to the trail by volunteering to help with trail maintenance. The SHTA will gladly provide you with information on how you can help.

The SHTA provides its members with maps, the *Ridgeline* newsletter, the opportunity to participate in the organized hikes and other activities, and the knowledge that through membership fees they are helping to preserve and protect a precious resource – the Superior Hiking Trail. For information on membership, SHTA activities, or trail maintenance or other volunteer activities, contact the SHTA office at (218) 834-4436, or at P.O. Box 4, Two Harbors, MN 55616-0004.

— ANNE MCKINSEY

A Superior Hiking Trail
Backpacking Primer

Backpacking allows you to experience the wilderness intimately and up close. While this chapter will help hikers enjoy the trail fully and with comfort, experience is the best teacher. Get out there and do it! The goal is to enjoy the walk *and* the camp.

General hiking tips

The Superior Hiking Trail is particularly well-suited to the novice backpacker. One is never far from the road, the grocery store and comfortable resorts if the weather or your enthusiasm turns, tempting you to bail out. Plan your trip accordingly. Plan escape routes to civilization ahead of time. Make your trip a combination of backpacking and resorting and enjoy the best of both worlds!

Regardless of whether you are hiking for a week or an hour, it is always a good idea to let someone know your plans. Tell someone where you plan to hike and when you plan to arrive; then check in when you return. The trail is not patrolled, so your safety or rescue in an emergency may depend on this common-sense precaution.

Backpackers will find back-country camping spots, most near a water source, every five to eight miles along much of the Trail, and the

Backpacker's camping equipment list

Personal items:

Sturdy, comfortable hiking boots

2-3 pairs wool socks

2 pairs liner socks, silk or synthetic

Long underwear

Wool or pile pants

Lightweight pants, shorts, short and long-sleeved shirts

Sweater or pile jacket

Rain jacket or poncho

Rain pants

Hat, gloves, gaiters if any probable snow

Bandanna, small towel

Swim suit
(same as shorts, perhaps)

Sleeping bag

Stuff sacks

Foam pad

Internal or external frame pack

Sleeping bag lash straps

state parks also have camping facilities. Additional campsites are planned in the future development of the trail. If a designated campsite is already occupied, bacpackers should move to the next site or ask to share the site. Although it is permitted to camp along the trail except where signs specifically prohibit camping, use should be concentrated at the designated sites. Within the state parks, camping is allowed only at designated campsites, and backpackers must register and pay regular camping fees.

Understanding the backpacker's checklist

The chief nemesis of the sore-hipped, aching-shoulder backpacker is, of course, weight. What to pack, how much to pack, and where in the pack to put it is often-requested information. Use the lists presented here for ideas of what to bring, not as a mandatory agenda. When all is packed, your backpack should weigh 30-50 pounds, no more! The use of lightweight gear may preclude using much of the camping equipment which you may already own. Use what you have that is lightweight, borrow from friends or rent the gear you need if you are unsure that this is the sport for you.

Following are some brief explanations of some items noted on the checklist.

Hiking boots. For safe packing and assured ankle support you will need lightweight over-the-ankle, lug-soled boots, preferably waterproof. Wet boots are usually sloppy fitting and lead to blisters and stumbles. Waterproofness is found in Gore-Tex (or similar) and full-grain leather boots.

Socks. The most important criterion is fit. Wear what fits well in your boots. A synthetic liner will "wick" moisture away from your foot. A wet foot is a cold foot. Wearing liner socks along with thicker wool socks helps disperse the friction which causes blisters. Let the socks rub against each other, not you.

Long underwear. Synthetic underwear keeps the wearer dry and warm. Leave the long underwear at home if you don't expect cool days or cold nights.

Sweater. Polyester or nylon pile sweaters serve the same function as a wool sweater. They keep you drier, are less bulky and weigh less than wool.

Rain jacket and pants. Make sure they work. At a minimum it should keep you dry when it's raining. Better yet, it should be something you can wear as an outer shell just to break the wind. In this case it should be a "waterproof/breathable" fabric.

Personal items, continued:

Compass
Map/trail guide/ map case
Water bottle or canteen
Eating utensils: cup, bowl, plate, spoon, fork
Sharp knife
Flashlight or headlamp, extra batteries
Waterproof matches, or butane lighter
Candle or firestarter
Sunglasses
Sunscreen
Insect repellent (mosquitoes, ticks, black flies)
First aid kit, with extra moleskin or foot care kit
Toothbrush, comb, biodegradable soap, etc.
50' nylon cord
Spare pack parts/ sewing items
Personal snacks or lunch food
Day pack for side hikes

Other pants, shirts, shorts. You should carry a minimum amount of these. You can change into clean clothes at the car.

Sleeping bags. Better quality down bags are very lightweight, low bulk, retain their loft for many years, and offer the greatest comfort range – from cold nights to hot, humid nights. Synthetic fill bags are heavier, bulkier, and offer less range of comfort than down bags, but will offer more warmth than a down bag when wet. They are not as resilient as down bags, tending to lose loft and warmth over time.

Stuff sacks. Use the one the sleeping bag comes in as a pillow filled with clothing. Use another inexpensive one for food, another for the cookset. Your sleeping bag should be kept in a truly waterproof stuff sack.

Pack. You'll need one that is capable of comfortably transferring most of the pack weight to and around your hips. Your legs should carry the weight, not your shoulders. This necessitates a comfortable padded hip belt. The shoulder straps should also be padded and fully adjustable so that you can readjust them as sore spots develop.

Tent. Again, anything will do but lighter is easier to carry. A freestanding design is desirable. Look for good ventilation features, durable construction, ease of assembly and sealed seams. With heavier tents, split the tent, fly, and poles among several people.

Stoves. Suffice it to say that a lightweight one-burner stove is desirable. Concern yourself with how easy they are to light, how well they simmer, how much and what kind of fuel they use, and how they work in cold or windy weather.

Food. Be prepared to carry lots of extra weight if you want to have fun making meals from scratch. The lightweight alternatives, freeze-dried foods, are very easy to prepare, and also relatively expensive. Instant cup of soups are inexpensive and very low in weight and bulk.

Lunch foods should be low in liquid content yet durable (oranges are heavy and full of juice, bananas bruise). Bagels can withstand heaps of abuse. Nuts, cheeses, salami, jams, peanut butter, cream cheese are all good bets. Also try high energy bars and fluid replacement drinks.

Breakfasts can be as simple as oatmeal or granola with powdered milk. Pancakes are labor-intensive but excellent if you don't need to get up and get moving quickly.

Water. All water must be boiled, filtered or chemically treated. Iodine tablets are the best chemical treatment but the water will taste of iodine. Back-country filters are considered to be the best option because they remove all harmful bacteria, giardia, and funny tastes. Look for self-cleaning and ease of use features.

Fun accessories. Some things serve little essential function but are fun to take along anyway. Bring one or two. Examples: boomerangs, Frisbees, Hacky Sacks, cards, games, harmonicas, chairs, books, solar showers, cameras, film, compasses, altimeters, etc.

Packing the pack. Get everything as close to your center of gravity as possible. When carrying 30 - 50 pounds this spot will be directly behind your spine and near your shoulder blades. Pack your sleeping bag at the bottom, heavier things behind your shoulders, and lighter things above your shoulders. Pack as little as possible to the far left or right of your spine.

No pack is truly waterproof. You should use waterproof stuff sacks for your gear and/or use pack liners (garbage bags work) or pack covers if you want bone-dry performance.

Backpacker's Camping Equipment List

Group Equipment:
Tent with rain fly

Tent stakes

Lightweight cooking stove

Fuel and fuel containers
(1 pt. per week
per person)

Fuel funnel (if necessary)

Cook set

Scrub pad,
biodegradable soap

Pot grippers

Community food
(lots of it)

Cooking grate for fires
(check current regulations
on campfires)

Water purification tablets
or water filter

Small trowel (for digging
personal latrines)

Backpacker's Camping Equipment List

Optional Equipment:

Lightweight shoes, sandals, or moccasins for camp use or fording streams

Waterproof pack cover

Extra tarp, cooking fly, emergency blanket

Binoculars (lightweight)

Star charts

Camera, film

Signal whistle

Thermometer

Altimeter

Notebook/pencil

Folding chair

Lantern

Fishing tackle

Games

Books

Toys

Bears and other raiders. Never take any food into your tent at night. Hoist all of your food and garbage in its stuff sack into a tree. It should end up hanging 10 feet off the ground and five feet from the tree trunk. Use a rock tied to the end of your rope to get the rope slung over a high sturdy branch, then tie the food bag to one end of the rope. Pull the other end until the bag is suspended, then tie off that end to the tree trunk. These precautions are worth taking although the more likely culprit which you will be frustrating is the resourceful chipmunk.

Synopsis. Backpacking can be as much work or as little work as you make it. If you can carry a minimum of extra frills your pack can weigh less than 30 pounds for a one-week trip and you will enjoy walking 10 miles or more per day. Or . . . you can bring all manner of heavy gear which allows for deluxe camping but sore shoulders after only six miles of walking. The perfect compromise is somewhere in between for most of us.

— RUDI HARGESHEIMER

Minimum Impact Trail Use

The Superior Hiking Trail *has been designed to minimally alter the* environment. It can be argued that its very existence, and this guidebook's encouragement of more discovery and usage of the trail, are detrimental to the wilderness ecosystems through which the trail passes. Conversely, the exposure of this pristine environment to a multitude of people may develop an increased awareness and appreciation of the environment for those people. Educating the public about wilderness values is, in fact, a goal of the Superior Hiking Trail Association.

Following is a reference list to help you minimize impact while on the trail. Read it carefully.

1. Proper planning

• Know the route and distance you will travel as well as the type of terrain.
• Try to use less popular routes to avoid overuse.
• Bring adequate food and equipment.
• Repackage most food into reusable containers so that unnecessary packaging such as cardboard, plastic, foil and glass stays at home.

2. Follow the rules

• Rules are made to protect the environment and make the wilderness more enjoyable for everyone.
• On the Superior Hiking Trail, signs may request that you stay on the trail in some areas. It may be an ecologically sensitive area or it may be private land where the owner has specified tht hikers stay on the trail as a condition of usage.
• Camp only in official campsites while in state parks (fees required).

3. Traveling

• Select proper footwear. Heavy "waffle stompers" cause much more trail damage than lightweight boots.
• Stay on trails. Switch backs and other trail features are there to prevent erosion and other damage.
• Do not take rest stops in areas that have sensitive soils, plants or animals.
• Travel in small groups whenever possible.
• Never blaze trees or leave other markers.

4. Making camp

• Use designated campsites whenever possible.
• Camping is allowed at designated campsites on a first-come, first-use basis. Camping in areas other than designated campsites is to be done at least 100 feet from the Trail and any water source.
• Locate your tent in a flat area with adequate runoff and do not trench around the tent.
• Avoid landscaping or otherwise "improving" the campsite other than removing sharp twigs and rocks from under the tent.
• Try to leave your campsite in better condition than you found it, by cleaning up any garbage.
• Never cut trees or other vegetation or pound nails into trees.

5. Cooking

• Try to use a stove rather than a fire. Stoves are easier, cleaner and more reliable.
• It is necessary to boil, filter or chemically treat all water for cooking and drinking.
• If fires are allowed, use only dead and down wood. Do not peel the bark from birch trees.
• Keep the fire small. Use existing fire circles. Drown the fire completely before you leave. Scatter or bury the ashes before you leave. Consider using a candle lantern instead of a campfire at night.

6. Clean-up

• Use even biodegradable soap as little as possible, or use no soap at all. Try cleaning the dishes with only hot water and a scrubby.
• If you do use soap, pour the soap water out on the ground at least 100 feet from any water source.
• Do not wash or bathe in any stream or lake. Use biodegradable soap only, washing and rinsing 100 feet from the water source.

7. Garbage

• If you pack it in, pack it out.
• Food waste, paper and fish entrails can be disposed of by burning them completely.
• Foil, plastic, metal and glass do not burn and must be carried out.
• Carry out trash that others have left.

8. Human waste

• Use established latrines wherever they are provided.
• The alternative is to use a "cat hole." Dig a hole 6-9 inches deep at least 100 feet from any water or trails and bury all waste.
• Carefully burn all toilet paper, or better yet pack it out.

9. Other people

• Keep your group as small as possible.
• Avoid loud yelling, loud songs and other rowdiness.
• Leave noisy pets, radio/cassette players, guns and other noisemakers behind.

10. Get together and help out

• Support environmental organizations.
• Join the SHTA and help maintain or build trails.
• Organize a group to clean up and/or repair damage in local areas.

MINIMUM IMPACT

The One-Car Hiker

An excursion on the Superior Hiking Trail can be as simple as getting to a trailhead and enjoying a simple loop hike or easy hike to a scenic spot. Below are some recommended loop hikes and day hikes that require no automobile shuttle.

Loops

Gooseberry State Park: Up to bridge on one side and back on another (page 60).

Split Rock River: Up one side, cross bridge, down the other side (page 64).

Crosby-Manitou State Park: Many loops, also hike to the SHT bridge or Manitou Cascades (page 92).

Caribou Trail: From the SHT parking lot along spur trail past White Sky Rock to Lake Agnes, then back along the Trail to Caribou Trail and hike on road to car (page 126).

Cascade River State Park: Follow side trails to Lookout Mountain, then return by "Hiking Club" trail along river (page 130).

Pincushion Mountain: Follow SHT either way around loop trail (page 146).

"Leg-stretchers:" One to three mile walks to scenic spots with no shuttle

Crow Creek and Wolf Rock from Castle Danger trailhead (page 54)
Beaver River from Lake County Road 4 (page 72)
Davis Drive Spur to Bean and Bear Lakes (page 76)
Highway 1 to "Fantasia" overlooks (page 84)
Lake County Road 6 to Section 13 cliffs (page 88)
Caribou Falls (page 98)
Sawbill Trail to Carlton or Britton Peak (page 110 or 116)
Oberg Mountain (page 120)
Cook County Road 58 to Devil Track River (page 146)
Kadunce River (page 156)
Lakewalk section (page 156)

In addition, you can hide a bicycle at one trailhead, drive to the next, then hike the Trail to the bicycle. To get your car, simply ride the bike back to it. Plan the bike shuttle so you can ride downhill (leave the bike at the end with the asterisk)! This arrangement works particularly well on the following trail sections:

Castle Danger* to Gooseberry State Park
Beaver Bay to Silver Bay*
Cook Co.Rd. 1* to Temperance River State Park
Arrowhead Trail to Jackson Lake Road*

48   ONE-CAR HIKER

Map Legend

Superior Hiking Trail

Spur trails or other trails

Parking areas **P**

Backcountry campsites ▲

Major campgrounds ▲

Reference points in text ◄

Main road ▬▬▬▬▬▬▬▬

Other road ▪▪▪▪▪▪▪▪▪▪▪▪▪▪▪▪▪▪▪▪▪▪▪

State highway |61|

Major county highway (39)

Forest service, township roads
or other county roads

NORTH *is always to the top of the page.*
SCALE 1" = 1 MILE
*The gridwork visible on the gray base map indicates
one-mile square sections.*

Two Harbors to Castle Danger

Start (End)
Two Harbors municipal campground

End (Start)
Silver Creek Township Road 617

Length of trail section
Approximately 9 miles, once completed

Safety concerns
• Some steep walking in Crow Creek ravine

Access and parking
Nearest Hwy. 61 milepost: 26.4

Secondary road name and number: none

Etc: Parking may be available in Two Harbors municipal campground.

Facilities
At starting trailhead (furthest southwest): campground with water, bathrooms, phone

Designated campsites on this section of SHT: none

Synopsis
Once completed, this hike will take you through some moderately challenging terrain. As of 1992, the first three and last two miles of the trail are completed. By early 1993 the entire section will be complete. The SHT winds along a rocky, pine-studded ridgeline in the northeastern half. The stunted trees and expansive views are reminiscent of a hike at timberline in the Rockies, with wide views of the pastoral Silver Creek valley.

Mile-by-mile description
(Mileage is approximate; section should be completed by July 1993.)

0.0 (9.0)
Hwy. 61
The first seven miles of this section follow a snowmobile trail for three miles, then depart from the snowmobile trail just north of the Stewart River. Note: The SHT passes through private land. Hikers are asked to be respectful of the owner's rights and stay on the SHT. No camping or fires on private land.

7.0 (2.0)
1992 terminus of SHT
A rock cairn marks the 1992 terminus of this section. There is a nice rock ledge below the cairn from which to enjoy the wide view of the Silver Creek valley with its sea of white pines and farmfields below. From here, SHT continues along a ridgeline, with views of the Silver Creek and Stewart River valleys, a relatively lush agricultural setting, across an old foot trail. The dwarfed spruces and pines and the mossy ground combine with the wide view to give this section the feel of hiking at timberline in high mountains.

5.5 (1.5)
Red pine overlook
Wide view from a red-pine framed outcrop into valley below. SHT continues over a ridgeline and down into a low, wet area with ash and alder, crossing a 20' footbridge and a small creek. Excellent deer and moose habitat in the mountain maple and cedar groves. SHT continues along a plateau, into a mixed maple forest and then through a tunnel of balsam.

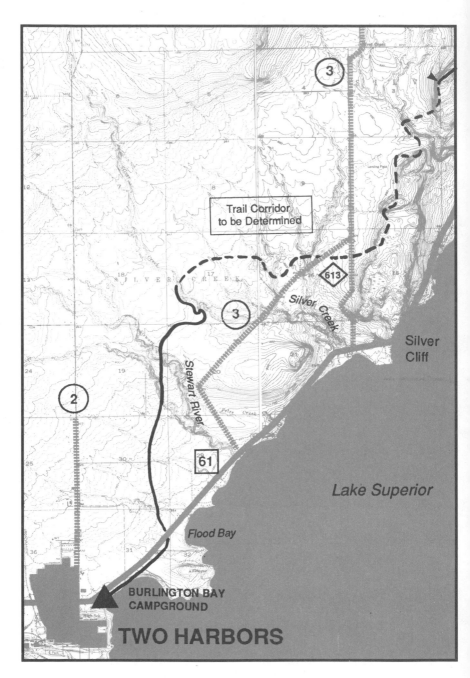

Trail Corridor
to be Determined

Silver
Cliff

Lake Superior

Stewart River

Silver Creek

Flood Bay

BURLINGTON BAY
CAMPGROUND

TWO HARBORS

TWO HARBORS TO CASTLE DANGER

Encampment Island

8.3 (0.7)
Overlook with bench
Scenic view across the Crow Creek valley, including pine-studded Wolf Rock prominent on far side of valley. SHT descends, sometimes steeply. This is private land, so please respect the owner's rights. Wooden steps lead into river gorge. Note the layers of rock along the cliffs of the creek. Each layer represents one lava flow, starting with smooth rock on the bottom of the flow and rough, bubbly rock on the top of the flow. A 40' footbridge crosses Crow Creek, then SHT climbs a talus slope, using a handrail at one point. There may be poison ivy on this slope. SHT continues through birches, across Silver Creek Road 617, then skirts base of Wolf Rock's dramatic cliffs for about 150 yards into parking lot.

9.0 (0.0)
Parking lot

Castle Danger to
Gooseberry Falls State Park

Start (End)
Silver Creek Township Rd. 617, north of Castle Danger

End (Start)
Gooseberry State Park interpretive center

Length of trail section
8.5 miles

Safety concerns
• Rocky cliffs at Wolf Rock – keep children in hand
• Deer stands along SHT – wear bright clothing in deer season
• Changing course of meandering Gooseberry River

Access and parking
Nearest Hwy. 61 milepost: 36.6. Intersection marked by SHTA sign.

Secondary road name and number: Lake Co. Rd. 106, which turns into Silver Creek Township (SC) 617 after 0.6 miles.

Etc: Go 2.4 miles on Co. Rd. 106/SC 617. Parking lot is on right.

Parking spaces available: Approximately 6 spaces at SC 617 parking lot. Overnight okay.

Facilities
At starting trailhead (furthest southwest): none

Designated campsites on this section of SHT: one — Gooseberry River

Synopsis
This section of the SHT has four distinct variations: the ridge between Wolf Rock and Mike's Rock, the low ground to the Gooseberry River, along the river, and in the state park. The two miles along the river outside the park are particularly charming, with beautiful fall colors, migrating waterfowl in season and great agate beaches.

Mile-by-mile description

0.0 (8.5)
Silver Creek 617 parking lot
SHT departs right side of parking lot, winds up through cliffs to the top of Wolf Rock. This may be one of the most dramatic first half-miles of the SHT as the SHT winds up to top of Wolf Rock with its pine-clad rock outcrops.

0.5 (8.0)
Wolf Rock
Great views at 1200' of the Lake, Crow Creek valley, white pine, etc. Note: SHT passes through a mile of private land. Hikers are asked to be respectful and stay on the SHT. No camping or fires on private land. SHT turns away from the valley as the woods alternate from open understory to dense growth. Lots of dead birch in this section, plus large mammal signs. Decomposed lava looks like gravel on the trailbed. SHT is wide with some mud holes when wet.

1.1 (7.4)
Side trail to vista
215 yards to vista overlooking Crow Creek valley. SHT continues along ridge, departing private land, through a cedar grove which is the source of a stream, and up and down some rocky spots. The woods alternate from open understory to a dense growth enclosing the SHT in a "green tunnel."

2.9 (5.6)
Mike's Rock
Vistas north and east to Gooseberry River Valley and Lake. SHT descends with stone steps past outcrops to low area of open birch and maple, crosses small stream and marshy area. Some dead birch in here, due to cumulative stress of recent years of drought, damage by birch leaf miner beetle and tent caterpillars.

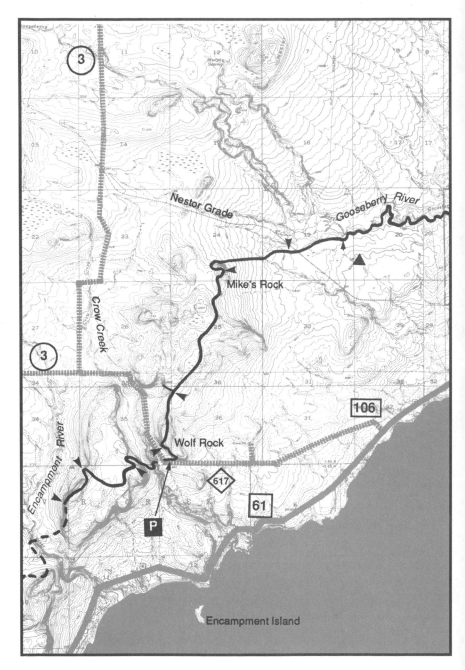

Nestor Grade

Gooseberry River

Mike's Rock

Crow Creek

Wolf Rock

Encampment River

106

617

61

P

Encampment Island

3

3

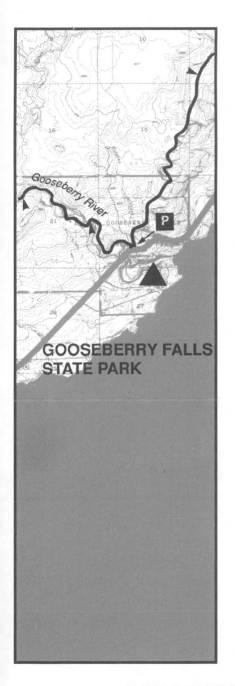

GOOSEBERRY FALLS
STATE PARK

Berries of the
Superior Hiking Trail

*Many hikers indulge in the
satisfying experience of eating as
they hike along the Superior
Hiking Trail. Several species of
berries are common along the
trail, and they ripen from July to
September. Blueberries are
frequent on the rocky outcrops
and scenic overlooks. These, as
well as other sweet fruit species,
need the full sun that is available
on the hill crests. But don't limit
your foraging to blueberries; keep
your eyes peeled for strawberries,
raspberries, thimbleberries, and
juneberries. Bring along a bag or
bucket — and remember, some
berries are poisonous so eat only
fruit that you know.*

4.0 (4.5)
Nestor Grade
Mid-point of section. This is an old logging railroad that was used for transporting logs to the Lake, and used now by ATV's. SHT climbs to higher, drier ground and a beautiful stand of birch trees. Berry bushes abundant, including raspberry and thimbleberry. SHT crosses several intermittent streams and reaches overlook on low area. Lots of beaver sign, including two very large beaver dams.

4.6 (3.9)
Gooseberry River and campsite
Note gravel meander bars along river – this is a good source of agates. Side trail 30 yards to campsite, marked by large spruce tree. SHT continues along river, an unusual setting due to meanders and ox-bow cutoffs. SHT subject to flooding as it alternates from flood plain to berm. These two miles of the SHT have no particular landmark, though look for an old fisherman's cabin at 6.0 (2.5) miles. This section is particularly beautiful in the fall and early spring. Many paths where beaver drag branches to water. Also, watch for migrating waterfowl in spring and fall.

> ### Gooseberry River campsite
> Tent spaces: 3-5
> Water: reliable, from Gooseberry River
> Setting: 30 yards off SHT
> Very high water might flood site

6.7 (1.8)
Junction with park ski trail
Wide, grassy ski trail follows river for a distance, past shelter and up the hill. Trail junction has arrows and "You are here" sign. Pass 10' fence which protects young trees from deer damage, called a "deer excloser." Spur trail leads to river and Fifth Falls. SHT follows along Gooseberry River cascades.

Gooseberry Falls State Park

Rocky Lake Superior shoreline and five waterfalls highlight Gooseberry Falls State Park. The park was established in 1933, and the Civilian Conservation Corps developed the park between 1934 and 1941, including the stone buildings, campground, picnic area, and trails. These structures have earned Gooseberry Falls State Park a place on the National Register of Historic Places. Today the park covers 1662 acres and includes a 70-site drive-in campground, a rustic group camp at the former CCC camp location, and 18 miles of hiking trails (including a self-guided trail along the Gooseberry River). The seasonal visitor center along Highway 61 serves as an interpretive center and nature store. Their selection of quality outdoor education material is unsurpassed in the area. Interpretive programs are provided during the summer and include guided walks, activities, and evening programs. A new visitor center is planned for the park in 1994.

7.8 (0.7)
Fifth Falls bridge
After crossing river SHT follows park's Voyageur Trail along east side of Gooseberry River, past gorgeous Fifth Falls.

8.5 (0.0)
Gooseberry State Park interpretive center

Gooseberry Falls State Park to Split Rock Lighthouse State Park

Start (End)
Gooseberry State Park interpretive center

End (Start)
Split Rock River Wayside on Hwy. 61

Length of trail section
6.0 miles

Safety concerns
• Unreliable water at campsite

Access and parking
Nearest Hwy. 61 milepost: 39.4

Secondary road name and number: none

Etc: Park at Gooseberry State Park Interpretive Center. Plenty of parking available. Overnight parking available next to campground on south side of Hwy. 61, with park sticker.

Note: This information is subject to change. Major park and highway renovations are planned.

Facilities
At starting trailhead (furthest southwest): bathrooms, outhouse, telephone, drinking water

Designated campsites on this section of trail: one — un-named creek

Synopsis
Trail starts out at a gentle climb through many birch, cedar, to higher elevation with lots of up and down, crossing bridges, past campsite to overlook with great views of Lake Superior including South and North Shores. Down to Split Rock River, along river to wayside.

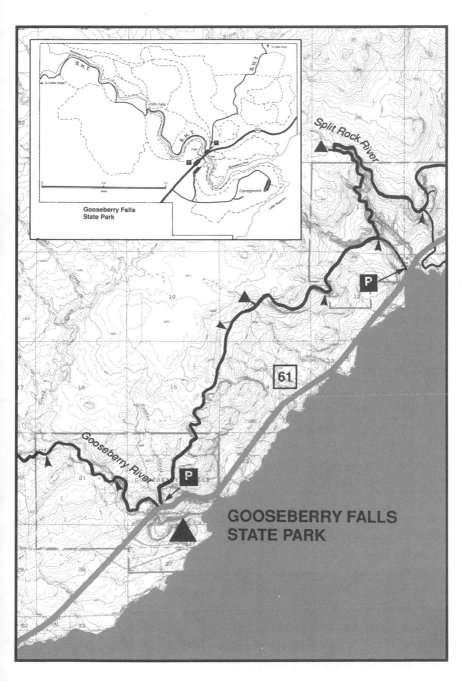

GOOSEBERRY FALLS STATE PARK

Inset map label:

Gooseberry Falls
State Park

Mile-by-mile description

0.0 (6.0)
Gooseberry State Park interpretive center
Trail follows state park ski trails through birch and pine, up a high rise and across Nelson's Creek. SHT climbs easily to park boundary, along 8'-wide trail with some wets spots. Well marked at junctions with ski trails. SHT goes under a cedar arch and through a cedar grove, onto private land.

1.2 (4.8)
SHTA sign
SHT goes through aspen, birch, and dogwood, follows park boundary signs, then crosses onto private land (as marked by sign) and a gentle downhill through aspen and cedar, then levels out in a cedar grove. Sign notes contribution of Philip Economon family. SHT follows base of rise on right, then crosses the Fire Mountain trail and five small footbridges across creeks. SHT departs private land and enters a stand of white pines.

2.8 (3.2)
Snowmobile trail
SHT crosses muddy snowmobile trail, goes through birch and poplar, across gravel logging road, across split log footbridge, then climbs small hill to cedar grove.

Public-Private Cooperation

We take things for granted sometimes. Like a clearly marked trail, or a footbridge over a low wet area. In fact, some things we almost can't help but take for granted because we never learn about them. For example, private landowners have helped make the Superior Hiking Trail a reality by sharing their property. More than 10% of the trail crosses land which is privately owned. Less than 1% crosses property of the Superior Hiking Trail Association. As you hike the trail, please remember that you are often a guest!

3.1 (2.9)
Campsite
Water supply in creek undependable for camping in dry periods. SHT goes through birch and pine and across small footbridge to an open area which is rocky and mossy, with good views of Lake – perfect for breakfast after staying at campsite, or to stop and smell the lichens. Be sure to follow rock cairns. Lots of influence of logging in these open areas, with obvious logging roads and small aspen under-growth.

> **Campsite**
> *Location: on un-named creek*
> *Tent spaces: 3*
> *Water: present but unreliable*

4.4 (1.6)
Bread Loaf Overlook
Last major overlook, on Lake and forest below, before descent into Split Rock valley. Up a steep grade and into Split Rock Lighthouse State Park (note sign). Easy descent through mature mixed hardwoods. SHT crosses two trails, passes through mixed pine and hardwood forest, then crosses another trail. Falls become audible below.

5.5 (0.5)
Waterfall and sign at trail junction
This is an un-named tributary of the Split Rock River. Sign reads "Gooseberry State Park 4.3 miles" (mileage is to Park boundary). Falls are worth a break for a granola or apple snack. At junction, go left to continue on SHT or right to Hwy. 61 (as the sign says).

6.0 (0.0)
Split Rock River wayside on Hwy. 61
SHTA sign in parking lot.

Split Rock Lighthouse State Park to Beaver Bay

Start (End)
Split Rock River Wayside

End (Start)
Lake Co. Rd. 4 north of Beaver Bay

Length of trail section
14.0 miles (For entire section. Distance is 10.6 miles if you start on east side of Split Rock River. Loop hike around Split Rock River is 4.4 miles.)

Safety concerns
• Occasional washouts along west side of Split Rock River

Access and parking
There are three distinct trailheads in this section:

1) Wayside rest on west side of Split Rock River. Milepost 43. 8 cars. Overnight okay for hikers.

2) XC trail on east side of Split Rock River. Milepost 43. Park on the old highway on the south side of Hwy. 61, no overnight parking.

3) Follow spur trail from Trail Center inside Split Rock State Park. Milepost 45.9. Overnight parking at Trail Center (permit required).

Facilities
At starting trailhead (furthest southwest): none
Services available at Split Rock Lighthouse State Park: bathrooms, water, phone, etc.

Designated campsites on this section of SHT: three — Split Rock River Crossing; west of Christmas Tree Ridge; and west of Fault Line Ridge

Synopsis
Split Rock River Loop:

This is one of the premier dayhike loops on the SHT. The attractive trail gently ascends the west side of the river which cascades down to the Lake. Some washouts, steep banks, occasional overlooks make this section moderately challenging and interesting as it courses generally 50 feet above the river.

The river cascades past cliffs and through clefts of sheer red rock walls draped with conifers. After crossing the bridge, the descending SHT affords some beautiful views of the river valley as a whole. When the SHT leaves the river it remains rather level until reaching a park shelter with a commanding overlook of Lake Superior and the river valley before a moderate descent along a spur to the highway about 1/3 mile northeast of the bridge.

Main SHT to Beaver Bay:

A challenging rocky trail affording dramatic views both to the Lake and inland. In many places the SHT follows along the edge of high escarpments with conifers clinging precariously 300 to 400 feet above the valley floor. There are many steep ascents and descents that take one through a wide variety of forests – much birch, maple, and aspen as well as impressive stands of cedars and white pines. The section also traverses part of the Merrill Grade, one of the historic logging railroads. Many sections of the SHT traverse long ridges of table rock, or follow long outcroppings which form walls for the SHT. In several sections one must proceed carefully along ponds bounded with large rocks and small boulders.

Split Rock Lighthouse State Park

Established as a park in 1971, today Split Rock Lighthouse State Park includes 1872 acres along Lake Superior between the Split Rock River and the lighthouse. The park hosts a number of historic sites including a commerical fishing village site, an early mine site, the site of a logging camp and dam, and of course the lighthouse and surrounding buildings. One of the unique aspects of the park is the cart-in campground. Campers cart in rather than drive in to the 20 sites located along Lake Superior. Four lakeside backpack sites are also available. Twelve miles of trails connect and follow the lakeshore and the ridge 600 feet above. Another popular pastime, fishing, especially for trout and salmon, is excellent along the Split Rock River.

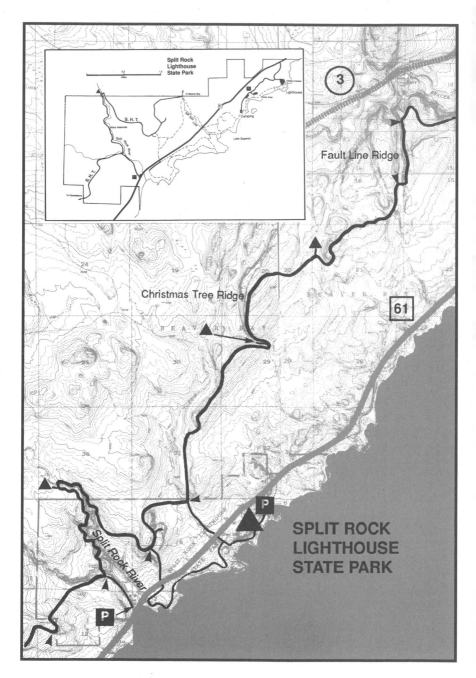

Split Rock
Lighthouse
State Park

S. H. T.

Split Rock River

S. H. T.

To Beaver Bay

Camping

Lake Superior

History Center

Picnic Area

Lighthouse

To Gooseberry

3

Fault Line Ridge

Christmas Tree Ridge

BEAVER BAY

61

P

P

Split Rock River

SPLIT ROCK
LIGHTHOUSE
STATE PARK

Geology of Split Rock River

The reddish-tan color of the rock in the Split Rock River gorge is quite a contrast to the more typical dark gray to black colors of the basalts of the North Shore. This rock, known as rhyolite, formed from a massive lava flow. As the flow cooled, it developed vertical cracks, or "columnar joints," similar to those at Palisade Head, as well as many smaller horizontal cracks. Post-glacial river erosion of the last 11,000 years, made easy by all these fractures, has eaten deeply into the flow, but has left some columns isolated right alongside the trail. Frost action over the centuries produces the "shingle" effect of loose chips and slabs on the rock surface and along the Trail.

Mile-by-mile description/Optional loop

0.0 (4.4)
Trailhead on west side of Split Rock River
Spur to SHT climbs gradually, with views of river valley to the east.

0.5 (3.9)
Junction with SHT
Waterfall just past junction of un-named tributary, also a semi-cave carved by the creek. SHT becomes more difficult after junction, climbing short, steep hills. Watch for washouts and steep overlooks. SHT winds through some impressive rock formations, including a chimney formation known as the Pillars. Many waterfalls are passed along the way. Watch for a large outcrop in the middle of the river which splits the flow of the river around a tree-studded island.

2.3 (2.1)
Split Rock River crossing
SHT campsite on west side of river, above bridge. East side of Split Rock River is more open, with conifers and bare rock. The river cascades through attractive red rock canyon walls topped with conifers. Partial views of Lake as SHT enters mixed birch/aspen forest. SHT reaches wide overlook, with view of Lake, highway, and lighthouse. Adirondack shelter marks junction with state park ski trails.

> ### Split Rock River crossing campsite
> *Location: on west side of river, just in from bridge*
> *Tent spaces: 2-3*
> *Water: reliable, from nearby river*
> *Setting: in grove of cedar*
> *Nice rock outcrop by rushing river*

3.9 (0.5)
Junction with spur
back to Hwy. 61
Follow spur trail back down to Hwy. 61 and finish loop. Spur trail is a XC trail but is maintained for hiking. This would be quite a ski run!

4.4 (0.0) Hwy. 61 parking lot

Mile-by-mile description/Main SHT

0.0 (10.6)
Trailhead on east side of
Split Rock River, on Hwy. 61
This trailhead cuts off about 3.4 miles and the River, described in the section above. Spur trail climbs up wide state park XC trails to junction marked with sign.

0.5 (10.1)
Junction with SHT
Turn right to head towards Beaver Bay, left for the loop described above. SHT follows ridgeline passing 2 good vistas of Lake and lighthouse (including spur 0.3 miles from junction), then descends. Some of the rock outcrops are old shorelines of Glacial Lake Duluth. The long gentle descent leads to a low, boggy area, then the junction with a ski trail, then crosses a creek on a wide ski trail bridge.

1.7 (8.9)
Junction with spur to state park campground
Soon after crossing creek, spur 1.4 miles from state park campground joins SHT. SHT soon joins old Merrill Grade railroad route. SHT follows moss-covered remains of old railroad ties through birch, aspen, and balsam. Watch for sign where SHT departs grade. SHT climbs to long walk along exposed rock ridge with spruce everywhere and rocks and moss on the surface and drop-offs to north. SHT crosses ATV trail at 3.0 miles. Large pines between SHT and view of Lake.

4.0 (6.6)
Spur to Christmas Tree Ridge campsite

Just west of campsite SHT follows 30' wooden stairway and crosses stream on split log bridge. After spur to campsite, SHT crosses logging road, then climbs to overlook atop Christmas Tree Ridge through open grassy area. Good views inland. SHT continues in open area, through a fine stand of white pines, and descends from ridge through brush and aspen, and past a pond. 50' boardwalk spans beaver pond area.

> ### Christmas Tree Ridge campsite
> *Location: on spur trail by creek*
> *Tent spaces: 3*
> *Water: reliable stream*
> *Setting: "grubby"*

5.6 (5.0)
Fault Line Ridge campsite

SHT passes large beaver pond, old logging camp, then climbs sharply to vistas of north and west. SHT follows rock promontories in a series of short ascents and descents. From ridge SHT descends steeply into valley and wet area.

> ### Fault Line Ridge campsite
> *Location: on spur trail*
> *Tent spaces: 3-4*
> *Water: yes*
> *Setting: beside beaver pond*

7.1 (3.5)
Fault Creek crossing

SHT crosses creek on split-log bridge, passes high mound of giant boulders, then traverses the rocky shore of a beaver pond. SHT climbs steeply through birch forest to Fault Line Ridge, formed by a geologic fault. SHT proceeds along east rim of fault valley, with dramatic views into a deep valley.

History of Split Rock Lighthouse

For a few centuries now, people have been trying to move safely along the North Shore of Lake Superior. The Superior Hiking Trail represents one of the first times people have tried to make it harder to get from Duluth to Grand Portage. Split Rock Lighthouse, which is visible from a number of points along the Trail, was one of many efforts to make the trip easier. Built in response to a particularly tragic year of shipwrecks (1905, with 215 lives lost on the Lake), the lighthouse operated from 1910 to 1961. The light was visible up to 60 miles away. Today, the lighthouse is owned by the State of Minnesota and is one of the most popular tourist sites on the North Shore, with over 200,000 visitors a year.

8.3 (2.3)
Fault Line Ridge overlook
From overlook, SHT turns east and follows cliffs above Beaver River. Views include the railroad tracks linking the taconite mines of Babbit with the processing plant in Silver Bay. Hikers can hear, and in season see, Glen Avon Falls on the Beaver River.

9.4 (1.2)
Spur trail
200 yards to view of Lake. SHT descends towards Co. Rd. 4 through birch, maple, and balsam forests, with groves of cedar in some low areas. SHT crosses a snowmobile trail which leads 1 mile into Beaver Bay 30 yards before road.

10.6 (0.0)
Co. Rd. 4 parking lot

Beaver Bay to Silver Bay

Start (End)
Lake Co. Rd. 4, 0.8 miles north of Beaver Bay

End (Start)
Penn Blvd., north of Silver Bay

Length of trail section
4.7 miles

Safety concerns
• Crossing of active Cyprus Northshore Mining Company railroad tracks

Access and Parking
Nearest Hwy. 61 milepost: 51.1

Secondary road name and number: 0.7 miles north on Co. Rd. 4

Etc: 6 spaces in lot off Co. Rd 4. Overnight okay

Facilities
At starting trailhead (furthest southwest): outhouses on Beaver River

Designated campsites on this section of SHT: none

Synopsis
The Superior Hiking Trail traces a serpentine route through one of the more developed sections of the North Shore, almost entirely within Silver Bay city limits. Despite the near-constant presence of taconite operations, highways, and towns, this section offers dramatic views as well as an intimate look at the Beaver River and its gorgeous falls. Easy access at both ends makes this a worthwhile journey, especially for the local history buff.

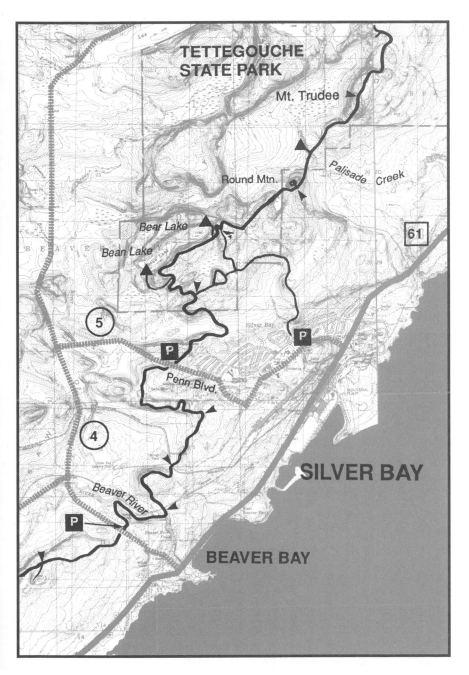

TETTEGOUCHE
STATE PARK

Mt. Trudee

Palisade Creek

Round Mtn.

Bear Lake

Bean Lake

61

5

P

Penn Blvd.

P

4

SILVER BAY

Beaver River

P

BEAVER BAY

Mile-by-mile description

0.0 (4.7)
Lake Co. Rd. 4 parking lot
SHT leaves lot along snowmobile trail (the Silver Bay Grant-in-Aid Trail) with wide views of valley, tracing beneath some settling ponds, and soon crosses Beaver River on a bridge shared by the SHT and snowmobiles. SHT turns down east bank of river immediately after bridge. This is a scenic river walk past groves of cedar and white pine, following the river as it changes from a gentle wide river to a roaring cascade. Near falls, SHT turns away from river and climbs through cedar, spruce, and birch to join the Betzler Rd. SHT turns left or north on the road. Arrow may be missing or inaccurate here.

1.1 (3.6)
Railroad tracks crossing
This is the main line bringing taconite to Cyprus Northshore for processing from a mine in Babbitt. SHT follows Betzler Rd. for another 100 yards, then at major intersection goes due north into a balsam thicket, then up a nice, fragrant stand of red and white pines to Sulheim's Overlook, a rocky knob with a partial 360° view of ridges, rivers, Silver Bay Golf Course, and taconite operations. SHT continues along cliff edge with views of tailings ponds and the pumping station below, then descends steep wooden stairs through a rock crevice.

2.0 (2.7)
Golf Course Rd. crossing
SHT crosses a jumble of roads, a snowmobile trail, and the double-barreled pipeline of the famous Milepost 7 operation. SHT picks up again in a grove of young aspens, immediately recrosses a newer dirt road, then leads gradually uphill to an overlook amidst red pines with views of Lake. This is the most remote feeling part of this section of the SHT, with little sense of the development around. As visible from the overlook, the forest here is a sea of birches with occasional towering white and red pines. SHT continues through this forest, up a

ridgeline, across an ATV trail and then up to a rocky open ridgeline.

3.0 (1.7)
View of Silver Bay, Cyprus plant
SHT follows ridge overlooking Silver Bay, Cyprus operations, Beaver River valley, Palisade Head, etc. Note unusual clumps of low, leafy bearberry and juniper. SHT winds along first ridge, past a spur to the nearby residential neighborhood of Silver Bay, then descends and climbs again to a second ridge, called "Blueberry Ridge" by the locals. SHT follows the Beaver River side of the ridge. From a clump of red pines one can look back to the parking lot on Co. Rd.4 where the hike began. A beaver pond below provides an opportunity for watching the busy ones at work. SHT descends into mixed woods, past a trail, through a wet area with ash trees, then gently up to one final rocky ridge before swinging down past a snowmobile trail to Penn Blvd.

Minnesota's Taconite Industry

Since the 1950's, the history and the landscape of the Beaver Bay area have been tied to the processing and shipping of taconite, a low-grade iron ore found naturally in deposits 50 miles inland. Reserve Mining Company built the world's first large taconite concentrating and pelletizing plant, creating the company town of Silver Bay. In the 1970's Reserve Mining drew criticism for its practice of dumping many thousands of tons of taconite tailings into Lake Superior daily. Following a 1978 federal court ruling, Reserve built the immense Milepost 7 tailings pond a few miles behind Beaver Bay. The tailings sludge is pumped through huge pipes from the Silver Bay plant. Reserve Mining Co. closed its Babbitt mine and Silver Bay plant in 1986. In 1989, Cyprus Minerals Co. bought the plant and reopened it on a smaller scale.

4.7 (0.0)
Penn Blvd.
Parking available here. SHT continues on other side of Penn.

Silver Bay to Tettegouche State Park & Highway 1

Start (End)
Penn Blvd., north of Silver Bay

End (Start)
Hwy. 1 (or Tettegouche State Park)

Length of trail section
10.7 miles

Safety concerns
• Trail often follows cliff edges, so use caution with small children. Steep downhills can be slippery in wet weather.

Access and parking
Nearest Hwy. 61 milepost: 54.3 (stoplight at Outer Drive)

Secondary road name and number: Outer Drive, 1.6 miles until it becomes Edison Blvd., then continue an additional 0.3 mile. Turn left onto Lake Co. Rd. 5 (same as Penn Blvd) and proceed 0.5 mile to roadside parking at signed SHT crossing. No lot, but plenty of parking on roadside. Overnight okay. New parking lot to be created with construction of Forest Road 11.

Davis Drive Spur: Take Outer Drive 0.5 miles from Hwy. 61 to Bay Area Historical Society parking lot on right. SHT spur leaves from far end of lot. Spur is also labelled "Twin Lakes Trail" (for Bean and Bear Lakes). Plenty of parking. Overnight okay with permission from Historical Society.

Facilities
At starting trailhead (furthest southwest): none

Designated campsites on this section of SHT: three — Bean Lake; Bear Lake; and Palisade Creek

Synopsis
This is one of the more challenging sections of the SHT, with lots of up and down, great views of the Lake and inland bluffs. It begins in the outskirts of Silver Bay and winds past beautiful Bean and Bear Lakes into Tettegouche State Park. The thick maple forests make it a popular fall colors hike.

Mile-by-mile description

0.0 (11.1)
Penn Blvd.
SHT departs parking area up rock stairway, crosses an ATV trail, past a sumac stand, across a gravel road (to Silver Bay's water supply), and then passes under a powerline into spruces. SHT then ascends ridgeline and crosses another ATV trail.

1.0 (10.1)
Series of outcrops with south and west views
Views over Silver Bay, water tower, Cyprus plant, and Lake. View at 1.3 miles of oak-maple-birch ridge. SHT climbs rock stairs. Green or blue paint on rocks marks SHT route, although these are not official markers.

1.8 (9.3)
Junction with Davis Dr. spur trail
One of two spurs to Davis Dr. SHT crosses footbridge, enters forest with maples dominating the low portion of the south-facing slope, then passes outcrops with oak and sumac. Lots of blueberries and juneberries in this part of the SHT. At one outcrop you can see back to the previous outcrop, and a beaver pond before SHT descends.

Sugar Maple Forests

The extensive maple forests of the Trail, which create much of the gorgeous colors of a fall hike, are the result of a lucky combination of ecological factors. Sugar maples require relatively warm winters and fairly deep soil to survive, both of which are rare in northern Minnesota. Maples can't survive below -40°. The thermal mass of Lake Superior keeps the north shore cool in the summer, but also keeps the area warm in winter. Maples thrive on the ridgelines, but not in the adjacent valleys, into which cold air sinks. The maple forests get their deep soil as a gift from two different glaciers which advanced parallel to each other, on both sides of the ridgeline, leaving enough glacial till on the ridges for this beautiful, out-of-place forest to thrive.

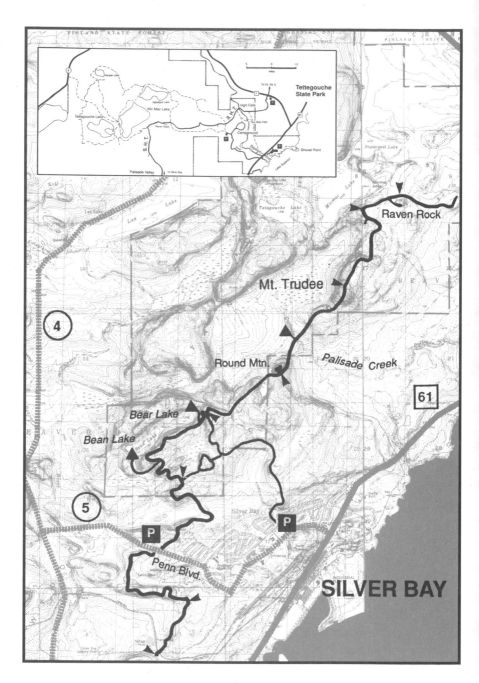

SILVER BAY TO HIGHWAY 1

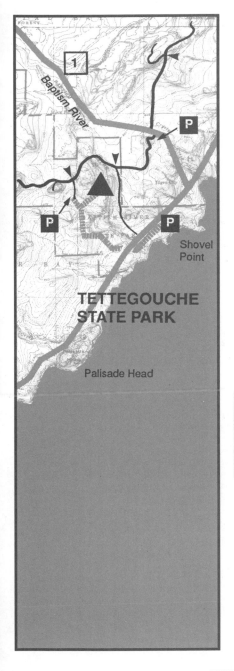

2.2 (8.9)
Bean Lake access trail junction
0.5 miles to Bean Lake and
campsite. Sign may have chew
marks from bears. Bean Lake is a
"Designated Trout Lake." Note
trail register at next overlook along
SHT, where SHT takes 90° turn.
From overlook look for Mt.
Trudee to the east, marked by
dark red pines. SHT passes
overlooks on Silver Bay, Milepost
7, and beaver ponds, but mostly
looks down on Bean and Bear
Lakes. The Bean Lake overlook is
impressive, with an open platform
of rock hundreds of feet directly
above the lake. SHT also passes
the remains of a log cabin, built by
local children in the 1950's.

Bean Lake campsite
Location: down 0.5 mile spur
Tent spaces: 3
Water: yes, from lake

3.4 (7.7)-4.0 (7.1)
Trail junctions
One spur to Bear Lake (3.4/7.3)
and rudimentary campsite. At top
of bluff, spur trail to Davis Dr.
(3.6/7.1) Then a snowmobile trail
to Silver Bay (4.0/6.7). SHT goes
through level maple-birch woods,

drops to an overlook of valley and view of Round Mtn. and Mt. Trudee.

> **Bear Lake campsite**
> Location: 150 yards off SHT
> Tent spaces: 1-2
> Water: from lake

4.8 (6.3)
Spur trail up Round Mtn.
1/4 mile trail to dramatic overlook on the expansive Palisade Creek Valley. SHT passes mature sugar maple forest and descends into Palisade Creek valley, crossing ATV trail, two split-log footbridges and a wet area with white cedars.

5.3 (5.8)
Palisade Creek
SHT crosses 25' footbridge over Palisade Creek. Good water source (treat before drinking). 300-yard spur to SHT campsite on east side of creek. SHT crosses ATV trail, climbs past a series of wooden steps through mixed woods to top of Mount Trudee.

> **Palisade Creek campsite**
> Location: 300-yard spur from SHT on east
> side of Palisade Creek
> Tent spaces: 2-3
> Water: yes
> Setting: streams east and west of site

6.3 (4.8)
Mt. Trudee
Mt. Trudee offers one of the SHT's best examples of a large, weather-resistant anorthosite dome. Its summit is picturesque, studded with pines. View north to 3 lakes, south over Lake, Tettegouche State Park headquarters. SHT continues along top of Trudee, with views

including Tettegouche and Micmac Lakes (named after lakes in Labrador, Canada), then descends through almost pure sugar maple forest. Forest changes to mixed maple-birch, starting at a series of rock walls alongside SHT.

7.5 (3.6)
Junction with state park trail
Park post with letter "L." State park trail goes 1.0 miles to Tettegouche Camp and Conservancy Pines. SHT continues on state park trail, first through pure maples, past mileage sign, and over a 40' plank bridge, then through low area and a copse of white cedars. A spur trail leads to good views from Raven Rock.

8.2 (2.9)
Junction with state park trail
Park post with letter "C." Tricky spot on maps. SHT descends through mixed maple-birch-conifer forest, past a 12' circumference white pine, then through "The Drainpipe," a 150' rock crevice with rock steps. SHT emerges into dominant birch stand being replaced by the spruce and balsam fir understory. SHT crosses another ski trail and leads through white cedar lowland. Look for spur trail up to view of Lake, Palisade Head, etc.

9.7 (1.4)
Junction with access trail to Tettegouche State Park trailhead parking lot
To access Tettegouche parking lot, turn on ski trail. 0.3 mile down-hill to parking lot, through a white pine grove, passing state park post "A." Straight on SHT through mature birch, across plank walkways. Watch for spur trail to state park campground. SHT descends wooden stairs past Baptism High Falls overlook, then crosses Baptism River on suspension bridge just above the falls. These are the highest falls entirely in Minnesota. The bridge, built in 1991 with substantial help from Minnesota Power, has a unique single-cable suspension design. This was by far the most elaborate and expensive bridge built by the SHTA. At trailside bench, look for spur trail to base of High Falls. SHT leaves river and goes up wood staircase.

Tettegouche State Park

Tettegouche State Park was established in 1979, and contains over 9000 acres of land, including six inland lakes and one mile of Lake Superior shoreline. Flowing through the park is the Baptism River and on it, High Falls, the highest falls completely in Minnesota. At the southwest corner of the park lies Palisade Head, a high bluff with a sheer rock face falling 200 feet into Lake Superior below. The park has 34 semi-modern campsites. The rugged, semi-mountainous terrain, and spectacular overlooks, make hiking on the park's seventeen miles of trails very popular. A one-mile self-guided trail to Shovel Point along Lake Superior educates as well as inspires. For the history buff, there is the Tettegouche Camp, a 1910 social camp. Its log buildings are currently being restored for group rentals. In addition, there is rich logging, maple syruping, and mining history throughout the park.

10.4 (0.7)
Junction with state park trail
Side trail follows river downstream 1.3 miles to park headquarters. SHT goes into birch woods and across a narrow roadbed. Two large white pines on the side, followed by a balsam fir "tunnel" for 200 yards. SHT leads through cedars, up a hill and along a ridge, then climbs 100-yard staircase. The large rock amphitheater is a former quarry site, the first quarry used in the first days of the 3M Company. Spur leads to SHT parking lot off Hwy. 1.

11.1 (0.0)
Hwy. 1

Wolf Ridge
Environmental Learning Center

---

*The Wolf Ridge Environmental
Learning Center (WRELC) facility is
a cluster of buildings with 1000 acres
of surrounding land which accommo-
dates hundreds of students, both
youth and adult. Wolf Ridge has been
at its current site since 1988, though
the program started in Isabella,
Minnesota in the early 1970's. The
well-regarded residential environmental education program has
introduced over a quarter-million
students to the wonders of the North
Woods; weekend programs offer a
wide variety of experiences for adults
and families. The trails on the
WRELC intersect with the SHT,
allowing for excursions onto the Trail
from the WRELC parking lot:
look for their marked turn-off a few
miles up Lake Co. Rd. 6.*

Highway 1 to County Road 6

Start (End)
Hwy. 1, 0.7 miles north of
Illgen City

End (Start)
Lake Co. Rd. 6, north of Little
Marais

Length of Trail Section
6.8 miles

Safety concerns
• On several sections the SHT
runs along the edges of cliffs
• Steep sections of trail slippery
when wet.

Access and parking
Nearest Hwy. 61 milepost: 59.3

Secondary road name and
number: Hwy. 1
Etc: Go north on Hwy. 1 0.8
miles. Parking lot on left,
marked with sign. Space for 6
cars. Overnight okay.

Facilities
At starting trailhead (furthest
southwest): none

Designated campsites on this
section of SHT: one —
Kennedy Creek

Synopsis
This section, one of the most
challenging, varies greatly from
easy, long stretches along the
contours to steep, scrambling
ascents and descents. There are
many open ledges affording
beautiful views of both Lake
Superior and its shoreline, and
inland lakes, mountains and
valleys. The trail is mostly dry
and winds through pockets of
maples.

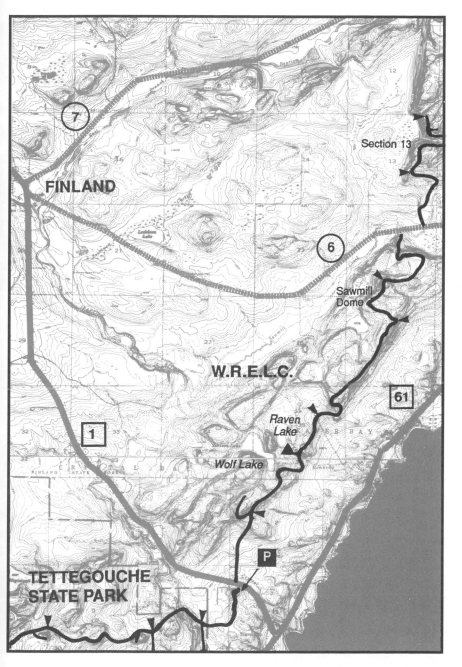

Mile-by-mile description

0.0 (6.8)
Hwy. 1
New parking lot built here in 1992. SHT crosses Crystal Creek and enters a May 1990 burned area of birch and aspen, with a sign. SHT crosses gravel logging road and traverses wet area. Note Sawtooth summits ahead. SHT soon climbs toward these summits.

0.9 (5.9)
Spur trail to overlooks
The overlooks begin 100 yards up the spur trail, 600' above Hwy. 1, the Lake, Palisade Head, Mt. Trudee, and the Silver Bay Harbor. Spur continues for 1/4 mile to more high bluffs. The adjacent land-owner calls this area "Fantasia," with vertical cliffs and a beaver pond below. SHT continues downhill from the overlook trail, levels out in a valley where it briefly shares an old road, then rises sharply to open ledges with view of Lake. SHT turns away from Lake, drops a bit, and then climbs switchbacks to an overlook above Wolf Lake, a beautiful lake deep in a depression, originally known as Johnson Lake. From the overlook, SHT curves around the peak, descends, then climbs again to a ridgeline overlooking the Lake.

2.3 (4.5)
Kennedy Creek campsite
SHT heads back into the woods to a campsite on north side of SHT. SHT continues across bridge, past spur trail which leads inland to Wolf Ridge ELC. SHT climbs to a small dome. Just before the steep section, a spur trail leads downward toward Lake. From the dome, SHT descends again.

> ### Kennedy Creek campsite
> Location: west side of creek
> Tent spaces: 5-6
> Water: from creek - reliable

2.9 (3.9)
Powerline
100 yards before powerline, SHT crosses old Johnson Lake Rd., also XC trail leading inland to Wolf Ridge. SHT continues and climbs to an expansive view of Lake, Fantasia, Mystical Mtn. and Marshall Mtn. SHT follows cliff line before it parallels the lake on a high ridge, with fleeting glimpses of Lake. Pass through two big rocks.

4.7 (2.1)
Overlook
From overlook, SHT turns sharply inland towards Sawmill Dome, and remains level and easy through maple woods. Just before the last rise to the top of Sawmill Dome, spur leads downward to a farm where owners may serve goat milk to thirsty hikers. Watch for their invitation on a trailside tree.

6.0 (0.8)
Sawmill Dome
This large cliff is studded with large pines and overlooks a maple forest, farmsteads, and buildings of Wolf Ridge ELC. Sawmill Dome and Sawmill Creek in the valley below are named after the turn-of-the-century Warren Sawmill in Little Marais. SHT skirts Sawmill Dome with steep cliffs, then descends sharply, past a spur trail (marked unofficially "to picnic place – rock overhang") which goes 150 yards to a semi-cave at base of cliffs. SHT continues to an overlook of Sawmill Creek valley, old Air Force radar base, and Co. Rd. 6, then descends. Climb briefly up log and rock steps to a hilltop with views of Lake and ridgeline. Descend past stone steps and wildlife opening.

6.8 (0.0)
Lake Co. Rd. 6
Parking lot is 0.4 mile east on Co. Rd. 6, in gravel pit. SHT continues on other side of road between this trailhead and parking lot.

County Road 6 to
Crosby-Manitou State Park

Start (End)
Lake Co. Rd. 6, north of Little
Marais

End (Start)
Crosby-Manitou State Park off
Lake Co. Rd. 7

Length of trail sections
2.2 miles (southwest end) and
2.7 miles (northeast end)

Safety concerns
• High cliffs near terminus

Access and parking
Nearest Hwy. 61 milepost: 65.3
Secondary road name and
number: Lake Co. Rd. 6

Etc: To reach the southwest
trailhead, follow Lake Co. Rd. 6
2.1 miles up from Hwy. 61.
SHT parking lot is on right in
gravel pit. 20-30 spaces in near
end of gravel pit. Overnight
okay. SHT trailheads are 0.1
miles and 0.3 miles west on Co.
Rd. 6 from parking lot. Directions for northeast trailhead are
the same as for the next section.

Facilities
At starting trailhead (furthest
southwest): none

Designated campsites on this
section of the SHT: none

Synopsis
These two short hikes lead to
some of the more impressive
terrain on the SHT, including
the high cliffs overlooking the
wide Sawmill Valley, popular
with local rock climbers and
known to them as "Section 13."
The climb out of the valley
shows the effects of valleys and
ridges on vegetation, as birch
and spruce turn into a nearly
solid maple forest.

As of 1992 a gap separates these
two sections. The southwest
section is a dead end. The
northeast section connects
Crosby-Manitou State Park and
Co. Rd. 7. The area within the
gap is privately owned and is not
to be trespassed.

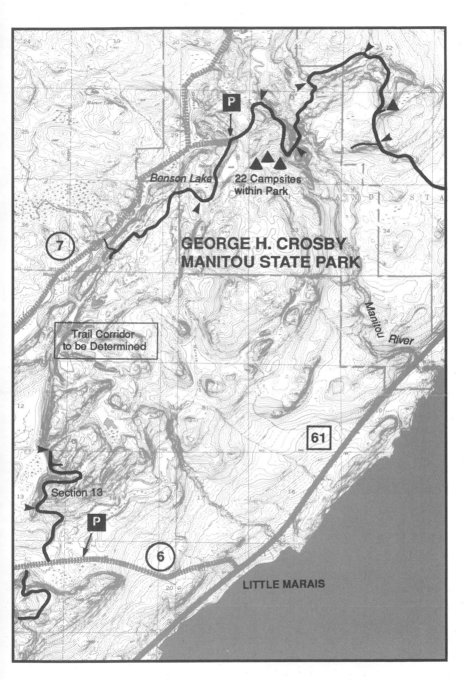

P

Benson Lake

▲▲▲ 22 Campsites within Park

⑦

GEORGE H. CROSBY MANITOU STATE PARK

Trail Corridor to be Determined

Manitou River

⑫

[61]

⑬ Section 13

P

⑥

LITTLE MARAIS

Mile-by-mile description

Southwestern end

0.0 (2.2)
Lake Co. Rd. 6
SHT departs from Co. Rd. 6 about 250 yards west of parking lot, and about 500 yards east of where SHT comes in from Hwy. 1 and Tettegouche. SHT enters dark spruce and birch forest, then across corduroy through alder. At creek crossing, currently a "Trail Under Construction – Dead End" sign. SHT climbs gradually along a fir- and spruce-lined ridge, past a beaver pond. At first there are scattered maples, but as the SHT climbs, the maples take over. This may be due to the cold valley air, which is too cold for maple, giving way to the warmer air on the ridges.

1.0 (1.2)
First outcrop/view
SHT climbs steeply to outcrop with view of valley, then continues up rocky ridgeline. Note the occasional oak trees, another sign of warmer microclimates on the ridgelines. The widest view comes at the open rocky ridge, a common rock-climbing area known as "Section 13." Views from here of inland ridges, beaver pond, and the old Finland radar base. SHT continues to another rock outcrop with a trail register, then descends into a cedar-filled gulch. SHT finally climbs to another set of views from a rocky, red pine ridge, including an impressive perspective on the Section 13 climbing cliffs.

2.2 (0.0)
Terminus
SHT ends in red pines and boulders. Plans call for connecting this section, as soon as possible, to sections beyond.

Northeastern end

0.0 (3.0)
Crosby-Manitou parking lot
SHT leaves from parking lot on state park's Benson Lake trail and follows west side of Benson Lake.

0.8 (2.2)
SHT leaves state trail
SHT turns to northwest along a typical Lake Superior Highlands ridge, including the maple forests. Watch for the "disappearing" lake to the east.

2.6 (0.4)
Fork in SHT
Fork to left leads within 1/8 mile to end of this trail section as of 1992. Fork to right leads down into the valley and across to Co. Rd. 7.

Crosby-Manitou State Park to Caribou River

Start (End)
Crosby-Manitou State Park, off
Lake Co. Rd. 7

End (Start)
Caribou River State Wayside,
on Hwy. 61

Length of trail section
8.1 miles

Safety concerns
• Deep gorges and cliffs at
Caribou and Manitou rivers.

Access and parking
Nearest Hwy. 61 milepost:
either 59.3 for Hwy. 1 or 65.3
for Lake Co. Rd. 6

Secondary road name and
number: follow either road to
Finland and continue north on
Hwy. 1 just past the junction
with Co. Rd. 6. Turn right onto
Co. Rd. 7, 8 miles to the
entrance of Crosby-Manitou
State Park. Approximately 30
parking spaces at state park
(state park permit required).
Overnight okay.

Facilities
At starting trailhead (furthest
southwest): outhouses, telephone, drinking water

Designated campsites on this
section of the SHT: many in
Crosby-Manitou State Park
(require sign-in and fee); one on
Horseshoe Ridge

Synopsis
This section of the SHT is quite
dramatic in terms of topography,
offering broad views of both
inland ridges, ponds, and rivers,
and of Lake Superior. The SHT
here is more rugged than most
sections and visits a variety of
forest habitats. The western half
of the section skirts the valley of
the wild Manitou River, while
the eastern half explores the
cedar groves of the Little
Manitou drainage and the
dramatic Caribou River gorge.

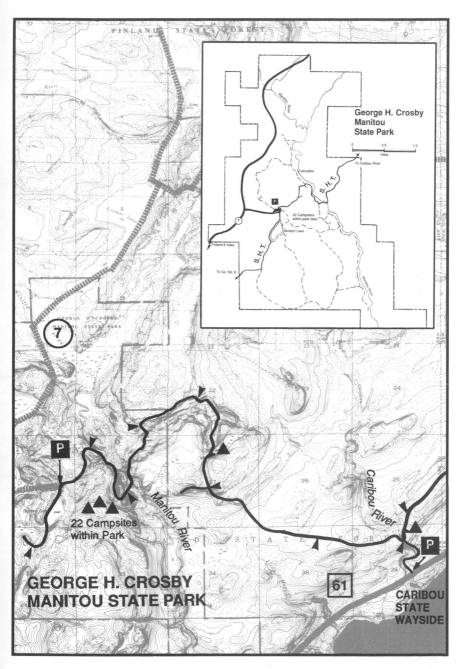

George H. Crosby
Manitou
State Park

0   0.5   1.0
miles

To Caribou River

22 Campsites
within park (fee)

Benson Lake

Finland 8 miles

To Co. Rd. 6

7

S.H.T.

S.H.T.

Cascades

Manitou River

P

P

22 Campsites
within Park

Manitou River

Caribou River

61

P

GEORGE H. CROSBY
MANITOU STATE PARK

CARIBOU
STATE
WAYSIDE

CROSBY-MANITOU TO CARIBOU RIVER   93

Mile-by-mile description

0.0 (8.1)
Parking lot

SHT leaves from parking lot at mapboard on the "Middle Trail," into semi-mature birch forest, past a large glacial erratic and across plank bridges. Spur on downhill side leads 70 yards to view of Lake and Manitou River valley. SHT descends steeply through cedars, past junction with Crosby Hill Trail.

0.9 (7.2)
Junction of SHT/Middle Trail with River Trail

Up-river from this junction about 1/4 mile are the Manitou Cascades, a worthy side trip. At junction, SHT goes downriver (right), past state park campsites 3 and 4, and up and over two bluffs with partial overlooks on river valley. Signpost marks where SHT goes downhill to the bridge, descending through a dark spruce forest and an overlook trail 100 yards before the river and bridge. The overlook allows glimpses through the forest of the tumbling river as it descends toward the bridge.

George H. Crosby-Manitou State Park

George H. Crosby-Manitou State Park is known for its rugged beauty and fine fishing. The wild and scenic Manitou River runs through the park on its descent to Lake Superior. George Crosby, an early mining magnate, donated the property for use as a state park with the provision that development be limited. With his wishes in mind the first back-pack-only park was designed. Today visitors camp at one of many remote backpack sites located mainly along the river. Hikers self-register for sites at the camping registration board near the camp office. There are 23 miles of trails, and fishing — especially for trout along the river or on Benson Lake — is among the most popular park uses. Because of the relatively undisturbed nature of the park it is common to encounter a variety of wildlife such as deer and moose, or less frequently, timber wolf, vole, mink, and pileated woodpecker.

1.6 (6.5)
Bridge over Manitou River
Manitou River is one of the most rugged river valleys along the shore. SHT runs steeply past white pine on east side of valley, then into scrubby mixed woods of fir, birch, and aspen. The climb is just 600 yards long but 300 feet up. SHT passes a series of four overlooks with views of the Lake and the Manitou River valley.

2.3 (5.8)
View of pond
After climbing short rocky slope, view pond and birch/balsam hill behind it. Look for a variety of lichens growing on the rock. Next overlook includes Lake and old Air Force radar base near Finland (white buildings). SHT continues along hilltop, alternating between maple woods and stunning views of the Lake. Note juneberry trees and sumac at the rocky openings. Beaver ponds are visible below. SHT eventually descends again into a deep fault line valley.

3.4 (4.7)
Beaver stream crossing on small beaver dam
SHT then climbs away from river through balsam, birch, and cedar. Forest changes over to maple, then birch and spruce. A series of overlooks on the Little Manitou, the Finland radar base, and spectacular maple hillsides. This area is known as "Horseshoe Ridge." Rock underfoot changes to crumbly rotting lava flow. SHT passes cedar and white pine. Spur near small footbridge goes to campsite, 150 yards.

> ### Horseshoe Ridge campsite
> *Location: near small creek on ridges overlooking Manitou River valley*
> *Tent spaces: 1-2*
> *Water: small creek near site and 400' down trail*
> *Setting: in a thick grove*

4.7 (3.4)
Spur to overlook
Spur leads 500 yards to wide view of Manitou, Little Manitou drainages, Lake, and ridges. SHT leads to another expansive view. Look for oaks on this long, rocky ridge. After descending and another view, SHT continues through cedar swamp with plank walkways. Look for logged-over open area – a good spot for birdwatching.

6.2 (1.9)
Logging road
Road built by Bob Silver for selectively cutting cedar in this area. SHT moves into birch/balsam woods, then a small rock outcrop and through spruces and bracken ferns. Between the logging road and the Caribou River the SHT crosses the historic Pork Bay Trail, a Native American and voyageur trail that led from Pork Bay nine miles inland to Nine-mile Lake. Listen for the Caribou River as the SHT descends. At the river the SHT turns left, up-river. Note deep gorge – great swimming for the adventurous.

7.3 (0.8)
Bridge over Caribou River
Trail junction on east side of bridge. Spur runs downstream to Caribou Falls and Hwy. 61 parking lot. SHT continues upstream to Cook Co. Rd. 1. Along spur trail, keep an eye on river as it cascades through narrow stone walls. Sign marks where spur trail forks, with the river-side fork going on narrow path down to gorgeous falls then downriver, the other fork straight to Hwy. 61 along top of bluff. Listen for the falls if you get confused.

8.1 (0.0)
Caribou Wayside
Mileage sign marks trailhead.

Bridges on the Superior Hiking Trail

Some of the Trail's most remarkable construction involves bridgework. Each stream that crosses the Trail is bridged, so hikers don't have to get wet or ford rivers. Approximately forty bridges of various length, material, and construction link embankments and landscapes. Although bridges are vital to trail layout, the best crossing is not always the most convenient place to build. A volunteer crew can make small wooden walkways from nearby resources, but some bridges are elaborately designed and need the transport of considerable lumber and other materials. The Baptism River suspension bridge, for example, required helicopter transport of supplies because of its complexity and location. Some bridges, like the one at Lake Agnes, were made during the winter, when larger timbers could be dragged across the ice. The Manitou River Bridge has a unique laminated stringer technique - at forty feet, this is the longest possible bridge with this technique.

Caribou River to Cook County Road 1

Start (End)
Caribou River State Wayside on
Hwy. 61

End (Start)
Cook Co. Rd. 1.

Length of trail section
9.0 miles

Safety concerns
• Floating bog at Alfred's Pond
• Active railroad tracks

Access and Parking
Nearest Hwy. 61 milepost: 70.5

Secondary road name and
number: none

Etc: Parking lot is on north side
of highway. Space for 10 cars,
overnight okay for hikers.

Facilities
At starting trailhead (furthest
southwest): none

Designated campsites on this
section of the SHT: four —
Caribou River; Crystal Creek;
on an unnamed creek; and at
Two Island River

Synopsis
After ascending the beautiful
and dramatic Caribou River
gorge, this section of the SHT
follows a series of ridges and
overlooks through mixed
deciduous woods. The bog
vegetation of the Alfred's Pond
area is a quiet highlight. Lots of
evidence of logging, including
roads and clearcuts, helps the
hiker understand the role of
logging in forest ecology.
Although this section is lengthy,
it is one of the easier sections to
hike — perfect for a long nature
walk.

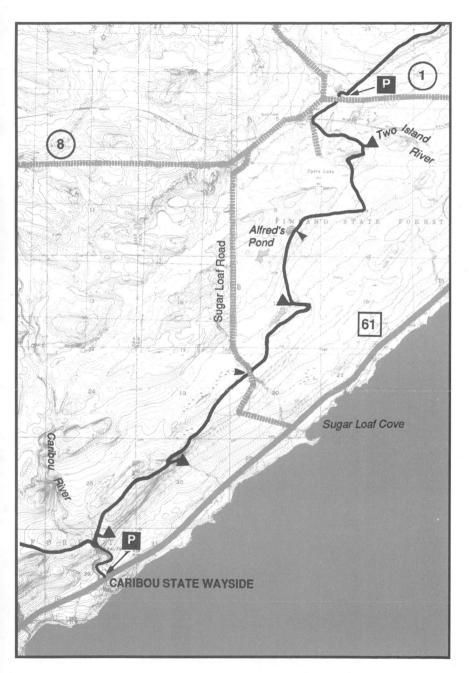

Mile-by-mile description

0.0 (9.0)
Parking lot off Hwy. 61
This is a spur trail which connects with the SHT above Caribou Falls. Spur trail leaves from north end of lot. Within 1/4 mile there is a trail junction. Right leads around falls directly to SHT. Left leads to base of Caribou Falls, then rejoins main spur trail at 0.5 miles. After two trails rejoin, spur continues along gorge of Caribou through pine and spruce.

0.7 (8.3)
Junction with main SHT
Note bridge across Caribou River. SHT across bridge leads to Manitou River. Spur trail to campsite just away from river. Past campsite SHT follows small stream, then through a clear-cut area.

> **Caribou River campsite**
> Location: up SHT from Caribou River, on spur
> Tent spaces: 3
> Water: from Caribou River

1.2 (7.8)
Logging road
Look carefully for SHT sign across road. Good view of Lake. SHT follows ridge, along logging road and then re-enters mixed hardwoods and birch forest after powerline, with seasonal view of Lake.

2.0 (7.0)
Spur to campsite
Right after campsite spur, SHT crosses Crystal Creek, then enters marvelous birch forest. If you want, follow Crystal Creek down a ways to a collapsed mine shaft. At this mine, note the wide band of calcite crystals in the bottom of the creek's gorge. These crystals led a prospector to believe there would be ore there also. SHT crosses powerline

and private road and passes through old Consolidated Paper plantations on private land.

Crystal Creek campsite
Location: down spur trail on west side of creek
Tent spaces: 1-2
Water: from small creek - may be dry
Setting: above creek in birches

3.5 (5.5)
Sugarloaf Rd.
After crossing road past parking lot and sign, SHT winds up and down ridge, with glimpses of the Lake, then an area with signs of an old fire. This is the most difficult hiking of the section. SHT enters mixed maple and aspen woods, then a swampy wet section.

4.9 (4.1)
Campsite, creek
SHT continues, across logging road and Alfred's Pond Rd.

Campsite
Location: near small stream, halfway between Sugarloaf Rd. and Alfred's Pond
Tent spaces: 1-2
Water: from creek, only in high water

Bogs on the Trail

Bogs are a type of wetland common in northern Minnesota, though less common along the Superior Hiking Trail. Bogs are characterized by a lush growth of sphagnum moss and high acidity. Since the bog is a nutrient-poor environment, some bog plants have evolved insect eating as a way of getting needed nutrients like nitrogen. The pitcher plant and sundew are two insectivorous plants common in the bogs in northern Minnesota. The sundew is a tiny plant usually found on the edge of the mat close to water. It has sticky tipped hairs on its leaves that trap insects. The pitcher plant is much bigger, perhaps a foot across, and traps insects in its hollow, fluid-filled leaves. Bogs are fascinating places to explore, but please use the boardwalk if provided.

5.8 (3.2)
Alfred's Pond
Look for bog plants like the carnivorous pitcher plant and sundew, as well as sphagnum moss, orchids, and blue-flag iris. Floating walkway built in 1992 allows one to see everything without getting wet or damaging the bog. After pond, there's some boggy walking. SHT climbs uphill, with possible view of Dyer's Lake through trees and, at 6.7 miles, of Lake Superior, then a steep downhill into birch valley.

7.9 (1.1)
Two Island River campsite
After crossing Dyer's Creek on a 35' split log footbridge, look for two forks on south side of SHT to campsite. SHT continues upstream on south bank of Two Island River, then ascends steeply through mixed conifers.

> **Two Island River campsite**
> *Tent spaces: 2-3*
> *Water: from river*
> *Setting: nice view of river, which is very accessible*

8.6 (0.4)
1st road crossing
SHT meets or crosses, in order: Dyer's Lake Rd, active railroad tracks which lead to Taconite Harbor, woods, Cook Co. Rd. 1, gravel pit road, Two Island River, then parking area.

9.0 (0.0)
Parking area off Cook Co. Rd. 1 (Cramer Rd.)

Wildflower Calender for the Superior Hiking Trail

May

Bloodroot	*Sanguinaria canadensis*
Violets	*Viola*
Wild Lily-of-the-Valley	*Maianthemum canadense*
Common Strawberry	*Fragaria virginiana*
Marsh-marigold	*Caltha palustris*
Spring Beauty	*Claytonia virginica*
Wood Anemone	*Anemone quinquefolia*
Goldthread	*Coptis groenlandica*
Nodding Trillium	*Trillium cernuum*

June

Starflower	*Trientalis borealis*
Bunchberry	*Cornus canadensis*
Columbine	*Aquilegia canadensis*
Mocassin Flower	*Cypripedium reginae*
Larger Blue-flag	*Iris versicolor*
May-apple	*Podophyllum peltatum*
Wild Sarsaparilla	*Aralia nudicaulis*

July

Meadowsweet	*Spiraea latifolia*
Spreading Dogbane	*Apocynum androsaemifolium*
Northern Bedstraw	*Galium boreale*
Indian-pipe	*Monotropa uniflora*
Heal-all	*Prunella vulgaris*
Cow-parsnip	*Heracleum maximum*

August

Goldenrods	*Solidago*
Large-leaf Aster	*Aster macrophyllus*
Fireweed	*Epilobium hirsutum*
Jewelweed	*Impatiens capensis*
Evening Primrose	*Oenothera*
Spotted Joe-Pye-Weed	*Eupatorium maculatum*

103

Cook County Road 1 to Temperance River State Park

Start (End)
SHT parking lot on Cook Co.
Rd. 1

End (Start)
Either Temperance River State
Park parking lot on Hwy. 61 or
SHT parking lot on Forest Road
243.

Length of trail section
8.0 miles

Access and parking
Trailhead #1
Nearest Hwy. 61 milepost: 78.9

Secondary road name and
number: Cook Co. Rd. 1

Etc: Go northwest on Cook Co.
Rd. 1 for 3.6 miles (first 1.7 miles
paved, rest is gravel). Lot is on
right 200' off Co. Rd. 1 and 0.1
miles before SHT crossing. Space
for 7-8 cars. Overnight okay

Trailhead #2
Nearest Hwy. 61 milepost: 79.1

Secondary road name and
number: gravel road directly

across from gas station in
Schroeder.

Etc.: Go 0.2 miles from Hwy. 61.
Park where road turns left, next to
electric substation. Space for 8
cars. Overnight okay

Facilities
At starting trailhead (furthest
southwest): none
Bathrooms, water, and telephone
at the gas station

Designated campsites on this
section of the SHT: three —
Fredenberg Creek; two at Cross
River Bridge

Synopsis
This section of the SHT offers a
comprehensive look at the steep
character of the region's watershed. The climb to Tower
overlook, the descent to
Fredenberg Creek, and the hike
along the marsh set the stage for
the highlight of the section, the
historic Cross River. Also, there is
ample evidence of both recent
and historical logging.

Mile-by-mile description

0.0 (8.0)
Parking lot
SHT has come 0.2 miles through the woods from crossing Co. Rd. 1. SHT continues from the left side of the lot. SHT passes through old clearcut area, then into the Northern Hardwood Scientific and Natural Area. Note conifers in low area on both sides. SHT climbs to Tower Overlook, with a beautiful view of Lake, then descends.

1.8 (6.2)
Fredenberg Creek
100' after footbridge, spur trail to campsite on south side of SHT, near sharp turn. SHT follows creek, then follows edge of marsh, known locally as Boney's Meadow. This is a wonderful place to view waterfowl. Look for moose tracks near marsh.

Fredenberg Creek Campsite
Location: spur 100' east of creek, site 200' from SHT
Tent spaces: 2-3
Water: from creek - reliable

Logging on the North Shore

Logging started on the North Shore in the 1880's, after pine forests to the east had been logged. Large stands of tall white and red pine were harvested, then transported by horse-pulled sleighs in winter and open waterways in spring and summer down to the Lake for transport to sawmills in Duluth and Ashland. The 1920's saw trucks and tractors bringing down black and white spruce for paper and lumber, and then secondary trees such as aspen, birch, and cedar for paper and other forest products. This fifty-year period of timber removal, transportation development, and human settlement drastically changed the woodlands along the North Shore. Following the depletion of the tall pines, the logging industry necessarily began sustained-yield logging to ensure renewable resources. The logged areas you see from the trail are part of a developing conservation movement emphasizing stewardship and recognizing the forest's timber, wildlife, and recreational qualities.

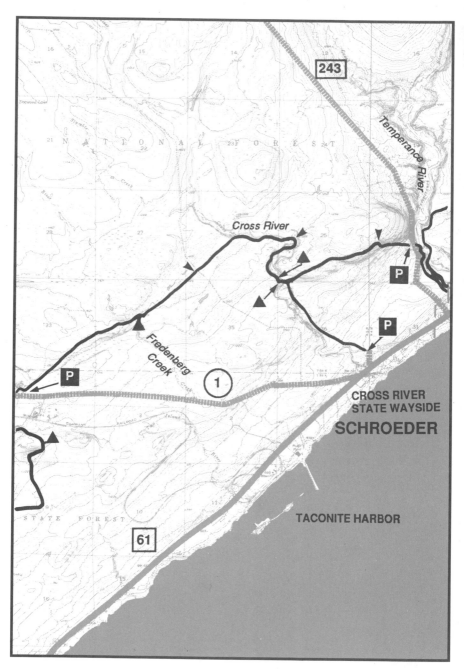

243

Temperance River

Cross River

Cross River

P

P

Fredenberg
Creek

1

P

CROSS RIVER
STATE WAYSIDE

SCHROEDER

TACONITE HARBOR

61

COOK COUNTY RD 1 TO TEMPERANCE

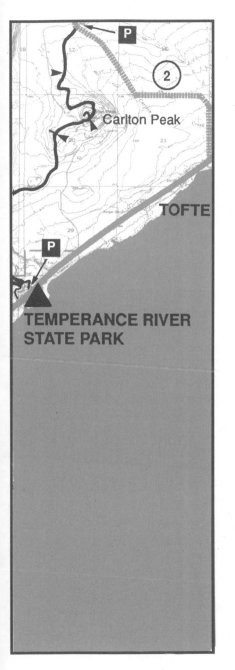

*Hugging the banks of this
spirited little river for over a
mile, the SHT gives ample
opportunity to observe the
various antics of the rushing
water – site of any number of
interesting historical events. The
Voyageurs portaged this stretch of
rapids to reach the calm head
waters, a chain of inland lakes,
and eventually Lake Vermilion,
near Tower. By the turn of the
century, loggers had entered the
watershed and used the river for
the roaring spring log drive down
to the boom at the mouth. This
included putting a series of dams
on the river. So "roaring" was
the river that there are accounts
of a bordello in what is now
Schroeder. The logging business
ceased operations in 1905 due in
part to a smallpox epidemic.*

2.9 (5.1)
Gasco Rd.
This is a historic logging road, also a spur to the North Shore State Trail, a multi-purpose trail linking Duluth and Grand Marais. SHT enters new-growth evergreens, probably an 80-acre clearcut replanted with white spruce in the 1970s, then a hardwood forest, then descends to a lowland. SHT then reaches the bluff of the Cross River.

3.8 (4.2)
Falls on Cross River
Great view of falls, excellent lunch or rest stop. The river is definitely the highlight of this section. SHT follows edge of river, up and down small bluffs. Look for beaver activity on sidestreams.

5.3 (2.7)
Cross River campsite and bridge
Note campsites on both sides of SHT. Trail junction after bridge: SHT goes straight, access trail 1.5 miles to Schroeder goes downstream. SHT follows bluff, then moves to ridgeline, with views of Lake and Taconite Harbor operations. Note the total absence of red or white pines, evidence of the pine logging operations early this century and their completeness. The large grove of mature red pine on this section was planted for future cutting.

> ### Cross River campsites
> *Location: 100' west of bridge, between SHT and river*
> *Tent spaces: 1*
> *Water: from river - reliable*
> *Setting: beautiful, easy access to river*
>
> *Location: next to bridge, 50' off SHT*
> *Tent spaces: 2-3*
> *Water: from river - reliable*
> *Setting: beautiful, easy access to river*

6.4 (1.6)
Top of ridge
Long and sometimes steep descent through a typical birch/aspen forest.

7.2 (0.8)
Temperance River Rd. (Forest Rd. 243)
SHT crosses road at parking lot 0.9 miles up Forest Rd. 243 from Hwy. 61. Either end hike here or continue along Temperance River into state park. SHT leads downstream as the Temperance changes from a wide, quiet river to a roaring cascade in narrow gorges. SHT alternates between woods and bedrock river edge. SHT eventually joins state park XC trail for about 0.3 mile, then turns sharply left to follow edge of second gorge for about 200 yards before reaching the snowmobile bridge across the Temperance cascades. Follow SHT downstream to parking lot, or upstream to Carlton Peak and beyond.

8.0 (0.0)
Temperance River State Park parking lot

Temperance River State Park to Britton Peak

Start (End)
Either the Temperance River State Park parking lot on Hwy. 61 or the smaller SHT lot 0.9 miles up Forest Rd. 243

End (Start)
Britton Peak parking lot on Sawbill Trail (Cook Co. Rd. 2)

Length of trail section
4.8 miles

Safety concerns
• At the base of Carlton Peak, use of hands is required to get through some large boulders.

Access and parking
Trailhead #1
Nearest milepost: 80.1

Follow Forest Rd. 243 0.9 miles from Hwy. 61 to SHT parking lot on left. Room for 6-8 cars, overnight okay, no services. Note: this is a good parking lot for hiking the SHT west to the Cross River and Co. Rd. 6. It's also a quiet alternative to the main Temperance lot on Hwy.

61 and leads you to the more private west side of the river, but makes the walk longer.

Trailhead #2
Nearest Hwy. 61 milepost: 80.3

Secondary road name and number: none

Etc: Trailhead is on north side of road, on east side of the river. Look for SHT sign

Space for at least 60 cars. 6 hour limit at parking lot, can park overnight at lot in campground area (need permit).

Facilities
Trailhead #2: bathrooms, outhouses, telephone, drinking water, campground

Designated campsites on this section of the SHT: none

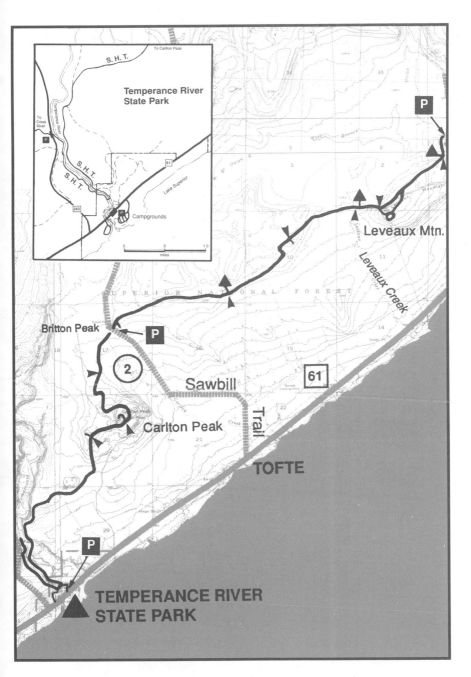

Temperance River
State Park

S. H. T.

To Carlton Peak

Temperance River

To
Cross
River

S. H. T.

S. H. T.

243

Lake Superior

Campgrounds

0   5   1.0
         miles

P

Leveaux Mtn.

Leveaux Creek

SUPERIOR NATIONAL FOREST

Britton Peak

P

2

Sawbill

Carlton Peak

Trail

61

TOFTE

P

TEMPERANCE RIVER
STATE PARK

Synopsis

This is one of the most easily accessible sections of the SHT and one of the most commonly used. The hike to Carlton Peak from either direction is an easy ascent, and the scramble to the top of the peak is a fun adventure with ample rewards of incredible views. Coming from Temperance River State Park, the hiker also gets to see the amazing Temperance River, with the roaring river deep in a dark basaltic canyon.

Temperance River State Park

The Temperance River was presumably so named because, unlike other North Shore streams, this river had no bar at its mouth. The 200 acres at the mouth of the river are now the State Park, which is best known for its deep, narrow river gorge, waterfalls, and the glacial potholes that dot the river valley. Fishing is popular on the Temperance and nearby Cross Rivers, where several species of trout and salmon have been stocked and have become established. Two campgrounds with a total of 50 sites are popular because of their lakeside location. Eight miles of trails connect with the North Shore State Trail, the SHT and Superior National Forest trails, and provide recreational use year around. Picnic sites are located along Lake Superior adjacent to the lower campground.

Mile-by-mile description

0.0 (4.8)
Trailhead at state park parking lot

This is a spur trail which joins the SHT at the snowmobile bridge 0.2 miles up the gorge from the trailhead. If you are coming from Forest Rd. 243, refer to previous section for first 0.6 miles. Spur and SHT follow "Cauldron Trail" up narrow gorge of river - look for interpretive signs. Trails fork and wander a lot, but SHT continues upstream until the river flattens out, then SHT becomes wide and clear. SHT joins XC trail at a switchback and climbs high on rim over river.

1.2 (3.6)
SHT leaves river

SHT enters scrubby woods, then a semi-mature birch forest. The Lynx XC trail follows the SHT. Look for signs of old white pines and fire. Two major fires have swept through here. Look for national forest survey lines, the wide straight cuts through the forest. At one point, SHT turns steeply uphill, leaving XC trail and climbing through birches.

Fire Ecology

Forest fires, either by their absence or raging presence, have had significant impact on the forests of the North Shore. Fire is a natural part of many ecosystems, providing a periodical cleansing and an easy way to return nutrients to the soil. Many of the birch forests along the Trail grew up following large-scale forest fires that followed logging in the area – as evidence, look in the even-aged birch forests for the numerous large fire-charred stumps of white pines. The few remaining patches of old-growth pines have likely survived a number of fires with their thick, corky bark and out-of-reach branches. The Trail's extensive maple forests, however, have thrived in part due to human suppression of fires; these northern hardwoods would not survive even a small forest fire.

2.6 (2.2)
Overlook spur
Look for sign and follow spur 80 yards for a view of Lake, Temperance River valley, and Taconite Harbor. SHT continues, through a solid birch forest, past a spur with an old access road and ski trail to Carlton Peak. SHT begins gradual ascent counterclockwise around Carlton Peak, through large fallen boulders. This is a popular rock climbing site and the only difficult hiking on this section.

3.1 (1.7)
Spur trail to summit
Well worth the trip to the top. Be sure to follow new trail. Trail register along spur in gulch, and spurs to main summit on left, secondary summit on right. Leaving the summit, there are high rock faces on left side of SHT. Watch for view of Britton Peak and Raven's Ridge above Tofte.

4.0 (0.8)
Lynx XC trail
SHT now in maple forest, then an open grassy area, created by the U.S. Forest Service by logging, raking, spraying, and planting spruce. Watch for kestrels, bluebirds, and migrating hawks. Lots of wooden walkways to cross muddy areas. SHT re-enters woods, crosses snowmobile trail, then crosses Sawbill Trail and winds into the Britton Peak parking lot.

4.8 (0.0)
Britton Peak parking lot

Carlton Peak

The high points on the North Shore landscape exist because they are made of rocks that have been more resistant to weathering and erosion over the billion years since they were formed.

Carlton Peak is a prime example, made of several huge blocks of whitish anorthosite rock. These blocks were carried or floated up from the base of the Earth's crust, 25 or 30 miles below, suspended in molten diabase magma. With very few natural fractures, these anorthosite blocks or "inclusions" also make up many of the knobs and hills in and around Silver Bay and Tettegouche State Park. A climb to the top of Carlton Peak reveals some tremendous views, which is why this was the site of a fire tower up until the 1950's (the foundation is all that is left of the tower).

Britton Peak to Oberg Mountain

Start (End)
Britton Peak access on Cook
Co. Rd. 2 (Sawbill Trail)

End (Start)
Oberg Mtn. parking lot on
Forest Road 336

Length of trail section
5.7 miles

Safety concerns
• Continual beaver activity west
of Leveaux Mtn.

Access and parking
Nearest Hwy. 61 milepost: 82.8
Secondary road name and
number: Sawbill Trail (Cook
Co. Rd. 2)

Etc: Go 2.7 miles north on
Sawbill Trail. Parking area on
right, 15-20 spaces available.
Overnight okay.

Facilities
At starting trailhead (furthest
southwest): outhouse

Designated campsites on this
section of the SHT: three — on
an unnamed creek; near a beaver
pond by Leveaux Mtn.; and on
the Onion River

Synopsis
This section crosses the
Sugarbush cross-country ski trail
system several times. The
section, one of the easier of the
SHT, begins as an easy, rolling
path through maple and birch
forest, with a carpet of leaves
underfoot in autumn. The
topography becomes more
dramatic in the central section
and the maple and birch give
way to spruce, balsam, and cedar
around the beaver pond. From
the pond the SHT ascends to
the Leveaux Mtn. loop and on
to the parking area. Wet and
seasonally wet ground is typical
along this section.

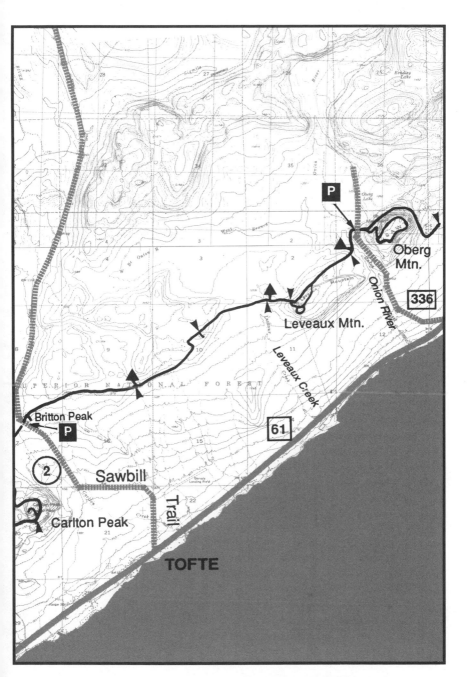

Oberg
Mtn.

336

Leveaux Mtn.

Leveaux Creek

Onion River

61

Britton Peak

2

Sawbill

Trail

Carlton Peak

TOFTE

SUPERIOR NATIONAL FOREST

BRITTON PEAK TO OBERG MTN   117

Mile-by-mile description

0.0 (5.7)
Parking area
Right after SHT leaves trailhead, spur leads steeply up to overlook near top of Britton Peak. The view from the top is dominated by Carlton Peak in the distance. There is a memorial for W.L. Britton, a WWII veteran who worked for the Forest Service for two years. His ashes were strewn on Britton Peak in 1947. The SHT crosses ski trails frequently, at 0.2. 1.2, and 1.4 miles. Ski trails have blue blazes, SHT has white blazes. Look for yellow birch curved into "S" shape. SHT also crosses numerous planks and corduroy in wet spots.

1.6 (4.1)
Wooden bridge
Look for signs of black bears chewing on bridge timbers. SHT campsite just east of bridge. SHT crosses XC trail, then climbs through young sugar maple stand to an overlook with a view of the Lake, Apostle Islands 30 miles away. SHT crosses old roadbed.

> **Campsite**
> Location: east of bridge
> Tent spaces: 4-5
> Water: from creek - unreliable
> Setting: no view at site, but one on rock above

2.9 (2.8)
Spur trail to Cedar Overlook
Steep 1/8 mile climb to view of Lake and Sawtooth Mtns., including Leveaux, Oberg, and Moose Mtns. SHT continues along ridge, then crosses ski trail. Forest begins to change to spruce and balsam. Lots of diamonds marking XC trails throughout this area.

4.2 (1.5)
Bridge across Leveaux beaver pond
Look for the beaver lodge to the north, and watch for moose. Beavers are active here, and as a result SHT may be flooded. SHT campsite 0.2 miles past bridge. SHT crosses snowmobile trail, enters cedar grove, then enters maple forest beneath the cliffs of Leveaux Mtn.

Beaver Pond campsite
Location: 0.2 miles east of beaver pond bridge
Tent spaces: 2
Water: use from beaver creek with caution

4.5 (1.2)
Junction of Leveaux Mtn. side trail
Side trail goes to top of Leveaux Mtn. for several typical grand Lake overlooks, also spur trail to Chateau Leveaux. The west end of side trail is steeper, rougher than east end. Leveaux Mtn. side trail rejoins SHT at 4.7 (1.0).

Trail Maintenance Volunteers

Is the trail too muddy for your tastes? Are more boardwalks needed? Is there a newly fallen tree that needs to be cut? The Superior Hiking Trail is maintained by us, the Trail users. If you or your group would like to lend a helping hand, let us know. Contact the SHTA to volunteer.

5.1 (0.6)
Bridge across Onion River
Campsite 0.1 miles past river.

Onion River campsite
Location: 0.1 miles east of bridge over Onion River
Tent spaces: 2-3
Water: from river
Setting: high above Onion River

5.7 (0.0)
Oberg Mtn. Trailhead

Oberg Mountain to Lutsen

Start (End)
Oberg Mtn. parking lot on
Forest Rd. 336

End (Start)
Lutsen Ski Area, on Cook Co.
Rd. 36

Length of trail section
6.8 miles

Safety concerns
• Steep overlooks on Oberg
Mtn.
• Steep slope on both sides of
Moose Mtn.

Access and parking
Nearest Hwy. 61 milepost: 87.5

Secondary road name and
number: Forest Rd. 336

Etc: Turn-off is marked by SHT
sign and XC ski sign, but is easy
to miss otherwise. Go north on
Forest Rd. 336 approximately
2.2 miles to parking area on left
side of road, opposite of Oberg
trailhead. 30 spaces available.
Overnight okay.

Facilities
At starting trailhead (furthest
southwest): outhouse

Designated campsites on this
section of the SHT: two —
Rollins Creek; and above the
Poplar River

Synopsis
This section has a bit of everything, from the scenic overlooks
of Oberg Mtn. and Moose Mtn.
to the dense maple forests of the
east end. After the optional
climb to Oberg Mtn., the SHT
winds through boreal forests of
birch, spruce, balsam fir, and
alder then climbs to the top of
Moose Mtn., where the views in
all directions are rewarding. The
ups and downs make this one of
the more challenging sections.
The last three miles go through a
rich maple forest before emerging at the gorge of the Poplar
River. This section was con-
structed by the Forest Service
and is one of the oldest sections
of the SHT.

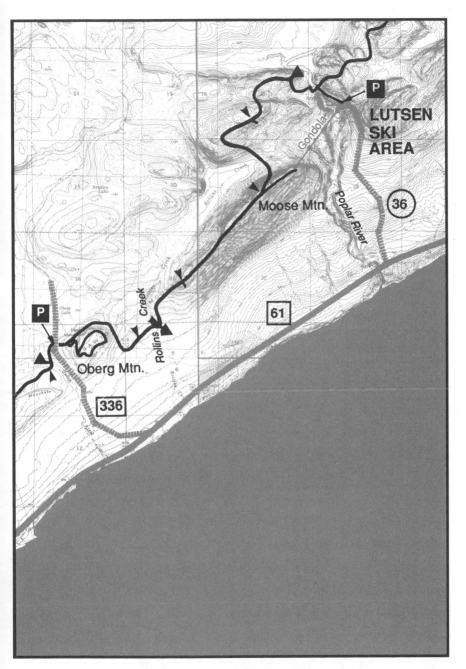

LUTSEN
SKI
AREA

36

Moose Mtn.

Gondola

Poplar River

61

P

Oberg Mtn.

Rollins

Creek

336

OBERG MTN TO LUTSEN   121

Oberg Loop

This is a 1.8 mile loop around the summit of Oberg Mtn. Oberg is covered by a rich maple forest, which gives out only at the many scenic overlooks. Work your way counterclockwise around the summit for about eight different overlooks in all directions, starting with Leveaux Mtn. and the Lake (and a distant Carlton Peak), then Moose Mtn., and finally inland to Oberg Lake and the rolling crests of inland ridges. Trail is well-maintained and overlooks are developed for safety. One of the overlooks has a picnic table. This is a great hike any time of year, but especially in the fall when the colors of this mountain and Leveaux Mtn. are at their peaks.

Mile-by-mile description

0.0 (6.8)
Oberg Mtn. parking lot
SHT leaves from opposite side of Forest Road 336, up some wooden steps. Trailhead is marked both by SHT sign and "National Recreation Trail" sign. Pass through a gate and past caution signs. Junction of Oberg Mtn. loop at 0.2 miles, a great side trip of about 1.8 miles (see sidebar). Follow SHT at junction, as indicated by the sign. SHT continues clockwise around the base of Oberg Mtn., through dense shrubs. Oberg Lake visible through trees to the north. SHT descends into wet area then crosses a creek.

1.2 (5.6)
Junction with XC trail
SHT goes straight across XC trail and also snowmobile trail. Mixed forest, with tall quaking aspen, a huge cedar tree, and lots of blue-bead lily. At one point in this stretch you can see Oberg Mtn. and pick out the shape of a human face high in the rock wall. Throughout this section the SHT is marked by white diamonds as well as the SHT sign. Just before Rollins Creek, spur to campsite.

> **Rollins Creek campsite**
> Location: *spur on west side of creek, 30 yards*
> *to campsite*
> Tent spaces: 3-4
> Water: *Rollins Creek - reliable flow*
> Setting: *cedar grove*

1.6 (5.2)
Plank bridge over Rollins Creek

SHT follows creek upstream a ways, then ascends from valley up flank of Moose Mtn., through yellow birch, cedar, and spruce, then paper birch, aspen, and fir. SHT gets steeper and steeper. Look for northern plants like shinleaf pyrola and twinflower near switchbacks on north side of Moose Mtn.

2.4 (4.4)
Southwest end of Moose Mtn. ridgetop

Short, unmaintained spur to partial overlook of Lake, Oberg Mtn. Moose Mtn. is 1688 feet above sea level and 1086 feet above the Lake. SHT winds along ridgetop, with partial views on both sides. Forest here is quite northern in composition, with spruce, birch, and balsam fir, and little undergrowth. Listen for the chatter of red squirrels. Maples only in low areas.

3.7 (3.1)
Spur to gondola

0.4 mile spur to northeast end of Moose Mtn., to Lutsen ski area gondola terminal and good views. A popular day excursion is to take the gondola to the top of Moose Mtn. and then hike the SHT back to the chalet, a total of 3.6 miles. SHT descends along north side of Moose Mtn. Descent is steep and rugged, with large basaltic outcroppings and a dark, shaded forest. SHT continues north, across plank bridge (headwaters of Rollins Creek, which SHT also crosses 1.5 miles to the SW), and enters thick, regenerating maple forest. Note all ages of maple trees, from seedling to mature. SHT slowly climbs.

5.2 (1.6)
Overlook

Small, unmarked overlook off side of SHT on Lutsen ski hills, gondola, and down Poplar River valley to Lake. SHT continues in maples, then forest changes to birch and spruce. 400 yards before campsite, spur to overlook marked by sign – to views of Poplar River valley.

6.2 (0.6)
Campsite

Campsite is just off SHT. Just past campsite is 10 yd. spur to overlook over marshy Poplar River, spruce swamp. SHT descends into wet area with scrubby alders, birches, thimble-berries, and raspberries. SHT turns onto XC ski trail (jct. marked by SHTA sign). SHT follows Poplar River gorge on wide trailbed, then crosses River on a wide bridge over a spectacular waterfall. Spur to parking lot goes downstream, SHT goes upstream on to Caribou Trail. Follow spur 0.1 miles to junction with dirt road, then another 0.1 miles to parking lot.

Ecology of North and South Slopes

Many factors lead to the particular kind of trees and other plants at any given point along the Trail. One factor that is often apparent along the trail is the difference between north- and south-facing slopes. Experienced hikers know the old wisdom that moss grows on the north side of trees. The same holds true for the ridgelines of the North Shore. Along the ridgeline, the forest on the southern or Lake side receives significantly more sunshine than the forest on the northern, inland side. This added sunshine makes the forest warmer and drier, an environment friendly to trees of the northern hard-wood type, such as birch, aspen, oak, and maple. The cooler, moister north-facing slopes have, in general, a more boreal feel, with spruces and fir, as well as the proverbial moss. Keep an eye out for these subtle changes!

Lutsen-Tofte
Tourism Association

Imagine having the task of promoting and marketing tourism in an area that is rich with rugged, beautiful landscapes featuring the largest body of freshwater in the world. Throw in recreational opportunities for all seasons. That is the job of the Lutsen-Tofte Tourism Association (LTTA). This organization includes most of the lodging accommodations from Little Marais to just east of the Cascade River. The participating businesses in this area offer a wide variety of accomodations from rustic to luxurious, and dining options range from a shore lunch picnic to white linen table cloths. The LTTA also offers lodge-to-lodge hiking packages along the SHT, allowing hikers to enjoy the best of both worlds; wilderness hiking as a backpacker would experience during the day, followed by fine lodging and meals during the night. Many resorts also offer shuttle service to trailheads and route information for their guests.

Poplar River campsite
Location: half a mile west of Poplar River right off SHT
Tent spaces: 3-4
Water: none - Poplar River nearest source
Setting: overlooking Poplar River valley

6.8 (0.0)
Lutsen ski area parking lot
Parking lot is adjacent to Gondola terminal.

OBERG MTN TO
LUTSEN

Lutsen to Caribou Trail

Start (End)
Lutsen ski area, on Cook Co. Rd. 36

End (Start)
Caribou Trail (Cook Co. Rd. 4), north of town of Lutsen

Length of trail section
6.4 miles

Access and parking
Nearest Hwy. 61 milepost: 89.8

Secondary road name and number: Cook Co. Rd. 36

Etc: Go 2.9 miles to end of road, past Alpine Slide, chalet and gondola terminal. Large "Bridge Closed" sign marks trailhead. Parking for 8-10 cars. Overnight okay.

Facilities
At starting trailhead (furthest southwest): bathrooms, telephone, drinking water

Designated campsites on this section of the SHT: three — two on Poplar River; one at Lake Agnes

Synopsis
This is a very pleasant and interesting segment of the SHT, with a diverse forest ranging from a mature maple canopy through mixed birch/aspen/pine and spruce to a small clear-cut. Stretches parallel the Poplar River and Lake Agnes, and there are several open vistas of the Poplar River drainage. In late summer it is a mushroom-hunter's heaven in terms of variety and supply.

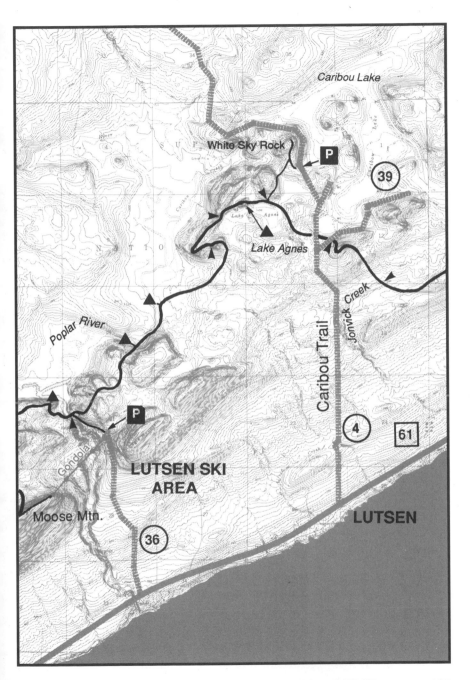

Caribou Lake

White Sky Rock

P

39

Lake Agnes

Caribou Trail

Jonvick Creek

Poplar River

P

4

61

LUTSEN SKI
AREA

Gondola

Moose Mtn.

LUTSEN

36

Mile-by-mile description

0.0 (6.4)
Trailhead for spur
Follow spur trail along old Co. Rd. 36 through mixed forest. Spur forks off old road to left. The spur soon meets the SHT by the wide bridge across Poplar River. SHT winds northeast through switchbacks to overlook on ski area. SHT then enters mature maple forest and gently rolling terrain. The SHT crosses a ski trail, then continues to Glove Overlook, a rock outcrop with views north and west on Poplar River valley. This area was the site of the 1990 Rainbow Gathering. SHT winds down through pine and aspen forest.

1.6 (4.8)
Poplar River west campsite
SHT follows river after campsite, crosses a snowmobile trail at 2.0 miles which has a bridge over the river, then crosses an XC trail. This area is heavily travelled by moose, so keep an eye out for tracks, antler rubs, and huge brown deer.

> **Poplar River west campsite**
> *Location: on a bend of the Poplar River,*
> *down short spur from SHT*
> *Tent spaces: 1-2*
> *Water: from river*

2.4 (4.0)
Poplar River east campsite
Lots of moose sign. Mostly spruce swamp for 1/4 mile, with SHT crossing many log footbridges. SHT leaves low area and ascends past small clearcut and into mature forest.

> **Poplar River east campsite**
> *Location: between SHT and river*
> *Tent spaces: 2-3 grassy sites*
> *Water: from river - reliable*
> *Setting: right on river*

4.0 (2.4)
Overlook on Poplar River
First of three overlooks on Poplar River valley. All three are good lunch break spots, with views of valley and river snaking far below, also of Lake. Mature maple forest.

5.0 (1.4)
Lake Agnes outlet bridge
Bridge built in 1989; note beaver dam. SHT climbs steeply to Lake Agnes overlook, with its trail register for hikers' entries. SHT descends to lakeshore and very nice campsite on lake.

> **Lake Agnes campsite**
> *Location: on Lake Agnes, right off SHT*
> *Tent spaces: 2-3*
> *Water: from lake*
> *Setting: one of the only sites on a lake*

5.6 (0.8)
Spur trail to parking lot
Sign clearly marks directions and mileage.
— Spur trail away from Lake Agnes 0.9 miles to Caribou Trail parking lot, past Cedar Hill, through a narrow rock canyon where a staircase has been sculpted from a single log, across a snowmobile trail, and up to White Sky Rock, overlooking Caribou Lake. Descend from there to parking lot.
— SHT crosses XC trail, Lake Agnes access road, then two more XC trails, through open forest and maples.

6.4 (0.0)
Caribou Trail

Caribou Trail to Cascade River State Park

Start (End)
Caribou Trail (Cook Co. Rd. 4)

End (Start)
Cascade River State Park, on
Hwy. 61

Length of trail section
9.4 miles

Safety concerns
• Crossing beaver dam at Jonvick
Creek is tricky — would recom-
mend use of hiking stick when
crossing. Only use canoe crossing
if you are comfortable with such a
craft.

Access and parking
Nearest Hwy. 61 milepost: 92

Secondary road name and
number: Caribou Trail (Cook
Co. Rd. 4) 4.1 miles up Caribou
Trail (pass SHT crossing at 3.1
miles) to parking lot for 5-6 cars.
This is also a public boat landing
for Caribou Lake. From here it's
1 mile on Caribou Trail to SHT
crossing, or 1.9 miles on the SHT
spur past White Sky Rock and
Lake Agnes.

Facilities
At starting trailhead (furthest
southwest): outhouses at Caribou
Lake boat landing

Designated campsites on this
section of the SHT: two — on
Spruce Creek and Indian Camp
Creek

Synopsis
This section follows along
ridgelines with many views of
Lake and inland ridges of
Sawtooth range. The variety of
habitats is as broad as anywhere
on the SHT, with everything
from mature maple forests to
dense groves of cedar, from a
massive beaver pond to wide-
open hillsides. It begins with a
moderately steep ascent but drops
gently to a valley and crosses a
beaver dam. It crosses two scenic
creeks and enters into the west
end of Cascade State Park.

Mile-by-mile description

0.0 (9.4)
Caribou Trail
SHT crosses ditch, past some corduroy and wet spots, and the climbing wall of the Cathedral of the Pines camp. Cross Co. Rd. 39. This land all belongs to the camp, so please no camping or fires. Moderate to steep climb through big cedar and maple to ridge with vista at left of Caribou Lake. 2 log benches are available for sitting and viewing lake. Many trails which are part of the camp intermingle with SHT. At 0.4 miles in, SHT turns down gentle slope through maple forest. Maples turn to alder thicket as SHT approaches Jonvick Creek and crosses some small plank bridges. Watch for woodcock near pond.

1.4 (8.0)
Jonvick Creek crossing
Beavers have built a dam at crossing site so you must either cross on the beaver dam or use the canoe if it's on your side. Consider use of hiking stick for balance. Immediately after dam, SHT crosses a wide, grassy snowmobile trail, then meanders through aspen. SHT crosses XC trail from Solbakken Resort, then rises up gentle slope through mature aspen to maple grove and views of Lake on top of ridge. SHT follows open area of young spruce (a Forest Service plantation) with wide views of Lake, crossing two dirt roads (one called the Hall Road), then re-enters maples. SHT continues along ridgeline in cedar and pine, with views of inland ridges, then descends. As with other ridges on the SHT, hawks are visible from this ridge during fall migration.

3.6 (5.8)
Spruce Creek crossing
Campsite on east side of bridge. SHT continues up through white pines and maples, across a snowmobile trail to another ridgeline with views of Lake and inland ridges, then slopes down to an open, sometimes muddy area and back up to another ridgeline with almost pure maple.

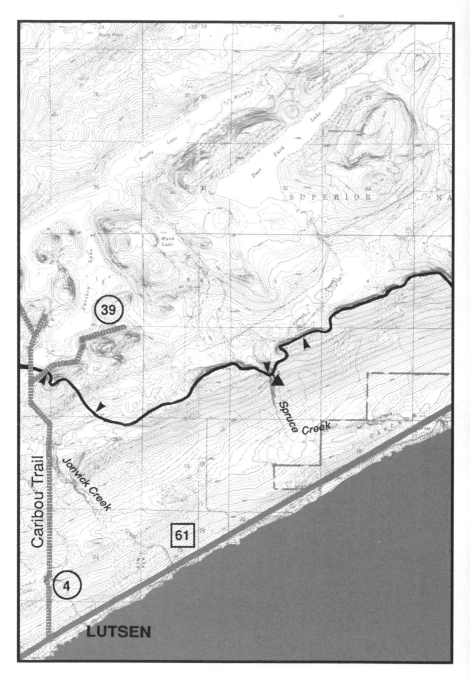

CARIBOU TRAIL TO CASCADE RIVER

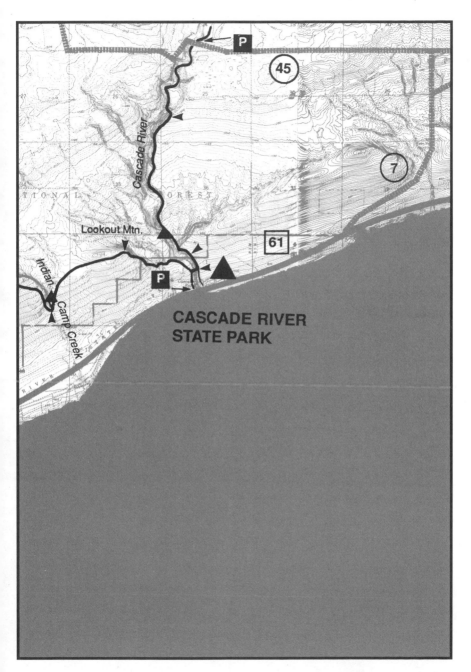

CASCADE RIVER STATE PARK

> **Spruce Creek campsite**
> Location: east side of Spruce Creek, just off SHT
> Tent spaces: 3-4
> Water: from creek
> Setting: in a dense cedar grove just above creek

5.2 (4.2)
Junction with snowmobile trail
SHT uses wider snowmobile trail for 0.5 miles, continuing up and down along grassy, open narrow ridge. Watch carefully as SHT leaves snowmobile trail sharply to left, then climbs ridge to view of inland ridges and the lakeshore toward Grand Marais, before descending along curving ridgeline and cliff edge, past 10-yard spur to viewpoint.

6.9 (2.5)
Indian Camp Creek
Campsite on east side of creek. SHT crosses a snowmobile trail, meanders through woods of cedar, pine and aspen, then down to wooden walkways across potentially muddy springs. Downed and dying fir are victims of spruce budworm infestation. SHT then climbs through aspen woods, meets state park XC trail and follows this trail past a state park trail map to junction with shelter, picnic table and outhouse. SHT forks off XC trail and heads up.

> **Indian Camp Creek campsite**
> Location: east side of creek
> Tent spaces: 2-3
> Water: from creek - reliable

8.1 (1.3)
Lookout Mtn.
Benches and a trail register at overlook. SHT stays left and descends, crossing XC trail to Cascade Lodge. SHT passes large stumps left over from white pine logging, then crosses another XC trail. Wooden plank

crosses a small feeder stream, and then SHT joins Cascade River State Park trail. SHT turns (left) onto XC trail soon after crossing stream, following State Park "Hiking Club" signs, past great views of one of the most photographed series of North Shore waterfalls. At the bridge over the river there is a platform for viewing the falls. The spur to the Hwy. 61 parking lot goes directly from the bridge down either side of the river.

9.4 (0.0)
Cascade River parking lot

Cascade River State Park

Named for the series of stair-stepping waterfalls on the Cascade River, Cascade River State Park offers numerous spectacular views along trails and bridges that follow and cross the river. Its 2813 acres follow a half-mile-wide band along 1 1/2 miles of Lake Superior shoreline. Cascade served as an Emergency Conservation Work (ECW) camp during the 1930's. Their handiwork includes the trails that follow the river. Within the park are eighteen miles of hiking trails, many of which hook up to the Superior Hiking Trail and other trails in the Superior National Forest. Located within the park is an enclosed picnic shelter, a modern campground with 40 drive-in sites, two group camp sites, and five backpack sites, one located along Lake Superior. A small picnic area is also located along the Lake.

Cascade River State Park to Bally Creek Road

Start (End)
Parking lot on inland side Hwy. 61 in Cascade State Park

End (Start)
Bally Creek Rd. (Forest Rd. 158)

Length of trail section
9.5 miles

Safety concerns
• Several steeper slopes can be slippery when wet, particularly on descents.

Access and Parking
Hwy. 61 Trailhead
Nearest Hwy. 61 milepost: 99.9

Secondary road name and number: none

Etc: Two parking options:
1) Park on north side of Hwy. 61, just southwest of Cascade River bridge. 8 spaces on Hwy. 61, 6 hour limit.
2) For longer or overnight parking, use the 2 small lots next to the shelter in the campground. There is a second trailhead here. Ask ranger for permission. State Park permit required.

Cook Co. Rd. 45 Trailhead
Nearest Hwy. 61 milepost: 101.5

Secondary road name and number: go 2.0 miles on Co. Rd. 7, left on Co. Rd. 44 for 0.5 miles, left on Co. Rd. 45 for 2.6 miles.

Etc. Park on right just before bridge. Lot holds 12 cars. Overnight okay

Facilities
At starting trailhead: bathrooms, outhouses, telephone, drinking water (all in state park facilities)

Designated campsites on this section of the SHT: two — both on Cascade River

Synopsis
After ascending the scenic Cascade River valley, this section of the SHT enters a long, remote area which includes the highest point of the SHT. The Hidden Falls section is a highlight, as well as the remote woods and tree plantations east of Co. Rd. 45.

Mile-by-mile description

0.0 (9.5)
Trailhead
Directly north of the Hwy. 61 bridge over the Cascade River, behind the guard rail. This is a spur trail and there is no SHT marker. Spur trail climbs up steps. Look for Cascade Falls below. Join SHT after 0.3 miles where SHT crosses bridge above gorgeous waterfalls. Spur from shelter trailhead in state park intersects SHT at footbridge. Stay on the east side of river. SHT climbs steeply, then levels off.

0.3 (9.2)
Trail junction
SHT turns off of state park hiking/ski trail. At this point, look for short spur to an overlook of the river. SHT descends, crosses feeder creek, then climbs back up bluff to campsite spur.

1.1 (8.4)
Campsite entrance
Just beyond campsite, SHT enters private land, as marked by sign. Be respectful of the owners' rights and do not camp, light fires, or go off SHT. SHT follows bluff above river, with occasional views and sounds of the river below. Note how tree mix along river differs from that along bluff.

> **"Billy goat" campsite**
> Location: *above river*
> Tent spaces: *1*
> Water: *from river 0.5 miles away*
> Setting: *steep hillside*

3.6 (5.9)
SHT returns to river
SHT makes steep descent to river's edge, climbs partway up bluff, and makes another steep descent to river (hiking sticks may be helpful, particularly if ground is wet). Note Hidden Falls and river

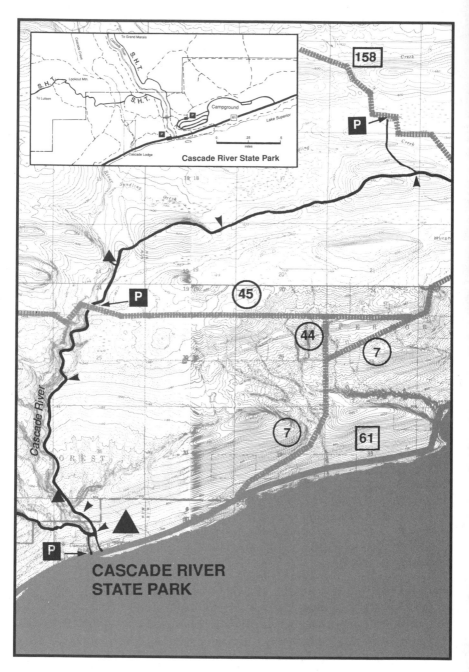

Cascade River State Park

158

P

45

44

7

7

61

Cascade River

FOREST

P

CASCADE RIVER
STATE PARK

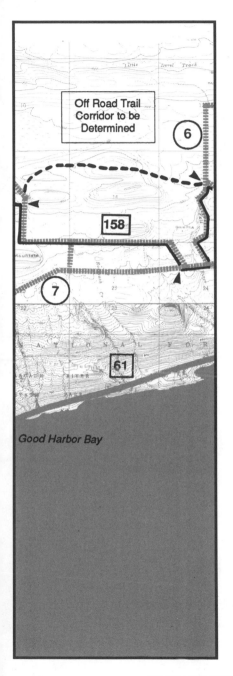

Off Road Trail Corridor to be Determined

⑥

158

⑦

61

Good Harbor Bay

Geology of
North Shore Waterfalls

The North Shore is blessed by many beautiful waterfalls, including several that give the name to the Cascade River. The abundance of waterfalls is basically the result of two factors: 1) the profound erosion of the Lake Superior basin by the great Ice Age glaciers, which led to the steep slope of the North Shore, and 2) the occurrence of hard igneous rocks underlying the coastal zone. The fast-running rivers have eroded the softer bedrock to form the deeper parts of the gorges. However, the bedrock has some harder parts, such as dikes or the lower parts of lava flows, and these resist erosion, leading to falls and cascades. Many of the falls on the Cascade River represent individual basalt lava flows.

cascades, a very picturesque area with several good rest spots. SHT departs private land as it continues along Cascade River through cedar, pine, alder and birch.

3.9 (5.6)
Co. Rd. 45 and parking lot
SHT passes under bridge, into parking lot, and continues from left side of lot entrance road, about 100' in from Co. Rd. 45. This area had a CCC camp in the early 1930s. SHT leads gradually along ridge, descends to cross a creek and then climbs steps to follow top of bluff along Cascade River. Note views of river and ridges to northwest. Generally an easy section to hike.

4.6 (4.9)
Campsite
At campsite spur, SHT turns sharply and moves away from river. SHT climbs gradually, passing through alder thickets, across planks, and through a stand of young red pine (whose needles carpet the ground) to reach a ridge overlooking the Sundling Creek valley. Eagle Mtn., the highest point in Minnesota, is visible from here. Note views across valley to north and government survey markers with "bearing trees" along side of SHT. Also national forest boundary markers. SHT descends past a series of cross trails and steps to XC trail.

> ### Cascade River northeast campsite
> *Location: down 75 yd. spur from SHT*
> *Tent spaces: 3-4*
> *Water: from river*

6.0 (3.5)
XC trail
SHT climbs low ridge and follows south edge of logged-over area. Note rapid aspen growth as the quick-growing tree sprouts from runners. SHT then climbs another ridge with several views back to Lake. SHT continues along several ridges though mixed forest to a high point on the ridge.

8.4 (1.1)
Spur trail
Look for sign at high point of ridge. At 1750 feet, this is the highest point of the SHT as of 1992. Spur goes north to Bally Creek Rd. (Forest Rd. 158) parking lot.

— Spur trail leads 0.7 miles to parking lot. Spur goes through birch forest, crosses a low area, climbs a low ridge and descends to travel a short distance along beaver pond on Sundling Creek. Beaver dam is visible from spur trail, but ignore cross trails beavers have made. Spur crosses creek on bridge, then follows a small ridge into parking lot.

— SHT continues along ridgeline through hardwoods with many views to north. SHT begins gradual descent through stand of young red pine, then descends to Bally Creek Rd. (Forest Rd. 158). No parking here, so dayhikers plan on hiking out the spur trail.

9.5 (0.0)
Bally Creek Rd.

Bally Creek Road to Grand Marais

Note: As of November 1992 the first half of this section follows county roads, in anticipation of future trail construction.

Start (End)
Bally Creek Rd.

End (Start)
Pincushion Mtn. trailhead north of Grand Marais

Length of trail section
9.1 miles

Safety concerns
• Traffic on road walk, cliffs on Sawtooth Bluff

Access and parking
Bally Creek Rd.:
Nearest Hwy. 61 milepost: 101.7

Secondary road name and number: Co. Rd. 7

Etc: Follow Co. Rd. 7 approximately 4.3 miles to a dirt road, then left for 0.3 miles to "T" intersection with Forest Rd. 158. Left on Forest Rd. 158 for 1 mile to bridge and SHT; parking area is on left another 1.5 miles along Forest Rd. 158.
10-15 parking spaces available.

Andersonville Rd.:
Nearest Hwy. 61 milepost: 109.3

Secondary road name and number: Gunflint Trail (Co. Rd. 12).

Etc. Take Gunflint Trail 1/2 mile north to Co. Rd. 7. Go west on 7 2.5 miles to Co. Rd. 6. Turn north for 1 mile to Andersonville Rd. with SHT trail sign. Turn east for 1/2 mile to turn-around.

No parking available

Facilities
At starting trailhead (Andersonville Rd.): none

Designated campsites on this section of the SHT: none

Synopsis
The western half of this section is currently the infamous "Road Walk," about 4 miles of dirt roads that detour around a future section of the SHT. This part is recommended only for through-hikers. The eastern half, about 4.9 miles, winds through the outskirts of Grand Marais, a level trail that passes an old ski area and fine vistas of the town and harbor.

Mile-by-mile description

0.0 (8.1)
Junction of SHT and Bally Creek Rd.
SHT follows Cook Co. Rd. 48 (FR 158) past Brazell's private drive-way, Brazell corner, and William's "T" junction.

2.4 (5.7)
Junction of Co. Rd. 158 and Co. Rd. 7
Continue east along Co. Rd. 7 0.3 miles to Co. Rd. 6, then north on 6 about one mile to junction with Andersonville Rd. Go east on Andersonville Rd. for 0.5 miles.

4.2 (4.9)
Andersonville Rd. trailhead
Road ends and SHT continues as foot trail from northeast corner of turnaround. Note: Private property on each side of turnaround. SHT immediately crosses junction of XC trail, then crosses elevated walk-way. Long nice walk on good well-maintained path through a mixed woods as the SHT is nearly flat and straight.

5.6 (2.5)
Junction with spur trail to Tower Rd.
SHT turns and soon passes 4-foot diameter white pine. SHT reaches Sawtooth Bluffs, with vistas of Grand Marais and harbor below.

6.3 (1.8)
Ski Chalet ruins
This was a local ski area in the 1950's and 60's. Spur trail leads north to TV towers and Co. Rd. 64. SHT stays below foundations, then soon crosses powerline and reaches more vistas of Grand Marais and Lake.

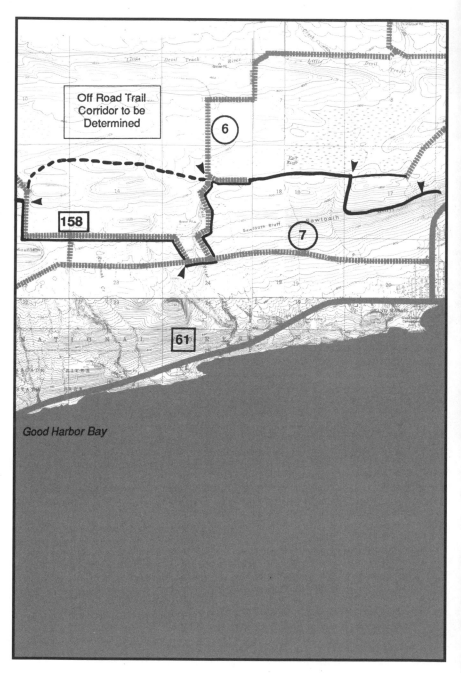

Off Road Trail
Corridor to be
Determined

6

158

7

61

Good Harbor Bay

7.1 (1.0)
Cross Gunflint Trail
No parking here, but road edge is wide and safe. This is the closest access to Grand Marais for services. SHT continues on other side and goes uphill, eventually joining a XC ski trail. Continue uphill (downhill leads to High School football field), across North Shore State Trail (snowmobile).

8.1 (0.0)
Pincushion Mtn. trailhead

Grand Marais to County Road 58

Start (End)
Pincushion Mountain area
trailhead, on Gunflint Trail

End (Start)
Cook Co. Rd. 58, north of
Hwy. 61

Length of trail section
4.7 miles

Safety concerns
• Cliffs close to trail edge at
Devil Track Canyon

Access and parking
Nearest Hwy. 61 milepost:
109.3

Secondary road name and
number: Gunflint Trail,
Co. Rd. 12

Etc: Go north on Gunflint Trail
1.7 miles, then turn east on
Co. Rd. 53 1/4 mile to trailhead.
Intersection at Gunflint Trail
well-marked as "Scenic Overlook." 15 parking spaces.
Overnight okay.

Facilities
At starting trailhead (furthest
southwest): outhouse

Designated campsites on this
section of the SHT: two — both
on Devil Track River

Synopsis
This is a 4.7 mile walk with an
optional loop to a panoramic
vista from summit of Pincushion
Mountain which includes the
town of Grand Marais. The
access to the town and services
make this walk quite convenient.
There are many side loops
available on the Pincushion Trail
System including the overlook.
Devil Track River crossing and
hike on canyon edge offer
dramatic views into the canyon
gorge.

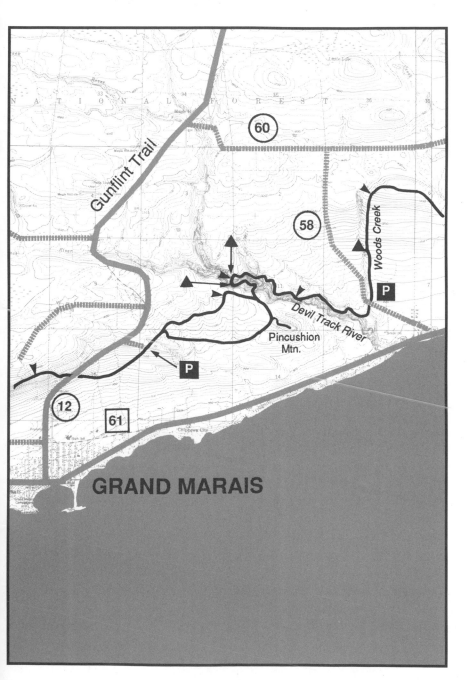

Gunflint Trail

60

58

Woods Creek

P

Devil Track River

Pincushion
Mtn.

P

12

61

GRAND MARAIS

Mile-by-mile description

0.0 (4.7)
Pincushion Mountain trailhead

This is a popular trailhead for XC skiing, with 25 kilometers of groomed trails. If hiking in winter, you must stay off the groomed trails which SHT follows for 2 miles. SHT passes a series of trail junctions marked #4, #5 and #6 within the first 0.6 mile, then #7 at 1.3 miles.

0.4 (4.3)
Junction #4

The SHT splits into two alternate routes around the Pincushion Mountain Loop. Turning left leads 1.4 miles along ski trails more directly to Devil Track River and beyond. Turning right leads to the spur trail to top of Pincushion at Map #8 and then to the river, approximately 2.6 miles. Summit spur leads 1/4 mile to summit for sweeping vistas of Grand Marais, Sawtooth Mountains and Devil Track River.

1.9 (2.8)
Junction of alternate routes

SHT departs ski trails and descends over 200 feet down to Devil Track River.

Cross Country Skiing and the North Shore Snowbelt

At numerous places, the Superior Hiking Trail intersects or shares its route with a cross-country ski trail.. Ski trails are wider than the Hiking Trail, tend to be grassy, and often have blue diamonds marking their course. The winter skier can have an experience similar to that of the summer hiker, with the same beautiful forests, dramatic overlooks and ease of access. There is an extensive network of trails that link all parts of the North Shore. The winter experience is made all the more enjoyable by the generally ample snow, created by the lake-effect snowfall along the North Shore ridgeline. It's not unusual to have two feet of snow inland and none along the highway. Note: if snowshoeing the Trail in winter, please stay off of any groomed ski track.

2.3 (2.4)
Devil Track River bridge
50-foot, "A"-shape bridge, built in the summer of 1992. The canyon
is deep and remote. Campsites on both west and east side of river.
SHT climbs uphill from campsite, about 0.2 miles to Spruce Knob,
then continues along canyon's edge, crossing split log walkways at 2.9
and 3.5 miles. Watch for scenic waterfalls and gorgeous red cliffs
below.

> ### Devil Track west campsite
> *Location: west side of Devil Track River at bridge*
> *Tent spaces: 1-2*
> *Water: from river*
>
> ### Devil Track east campsite
> *Location: east side of Devil Track River upstream*
> *from bridge*
> *Tent spaces: 1-2*
> *Water: from river*

3.7 (1.0)
Barrier Falls overlook
Deep vista into canyon. SHT passes 1937 tree plantation marker, and
eventually descends cedar steps to cross small stream on bridge, which
descends several vertical drops as it carves its way to the river. SHT
continues through pine plantation. A fisherman's trail crosses the
SHT and heads straight down to river. About 0.2 miles from parking
lot is last (or first) good overlook on canyon.

4.7 (0.0)
Cook Co. Rd. 58

County Road 58 to Kadunce River

Start (End)
Cook Co. Rd. 58

End (Start)
Kadunce River Wayside on Hwy. 61

Length of trail section
9.2 miles

Access and parking
Co. Rd. 58:
Nearest Hwy. 61 milepost: 113.8

Secondary road name and number: Co. Rd. 58

Etc: Go north on Co. Rd. 58 0.8 miles. Parking along side of road (pullover) for 6 cars. Overnight okay.

Co. Rd. 14:
Nearest Hwy. 61 milepost: 117.6

Secondary road name and number: Co. Rd 14.

Etc: Go 0.7 mile from Hwy. 61. Lot holds 8 cars, overnight okay.

Facilities
At starting trailhead (furthest southwest): none

Designated campsites on this section of the SHT: four — Wood's Creek; Cliff Creek; Durfee Creek; Crow Creek

Synopsis
There are a number of unusual features to this section of the SHT. The section begins and ends with intimate streams, from the gentle gurgle of Wood's Creek to the deep gorges of the Kadunce River, which offer a fascinating glimpse into the region's geology. The middle part of the section takes you across a unique high, wet area with over two dozen footbridges. Unusual trees on this section include red oak and black spruce.

Mile-by-mile description

0.0 (9.2)
Parking lot on Co. Rd. 58
SHT begins in red pines on east side of Wood's Creek, a feeder stream to the Devil Track River, then follows bouldery stream through birch, aspen and ash. The sharp-edged red rock is rhyolite. SHT then goes through dark spruces with old man's beard (a lichen) drooping from branches.

> **Wood's Creek campsite**
> *Location: east side of Wood's Creek*
> *Tent spaces: 2-3*
> *Water: from creek*

1.2 (8.0)
SHT leaves creek
SHT turns east and climbs into park-like birch forest, then a series of cutovers and open areas (SHT marked by rock cairns). Views of Lake, Pincushion Mtn. at first, then wide view to southwest of Pincushion, Maple Hill radio tower, and Sawtooth range. Birches gradually give way to aspens. In the open area, watch for bluebirds in the field and Five-Mile Rock in the Lake. At far side of field, SHT enters a mixed woods, crosses a trail, then passes through a wildlife opening.

3.0 (6.2)
Durfee Creek campsite
After campsite, SHT crosses a series of over 20 plank bridges in this up-and-down section, with lots of black spruce and burned stumps.

> **Durfee Creek campsite**
> *Location: west side of Durfee Creek*
> *Tent spaces: 1-2*
> *Water: from creek*

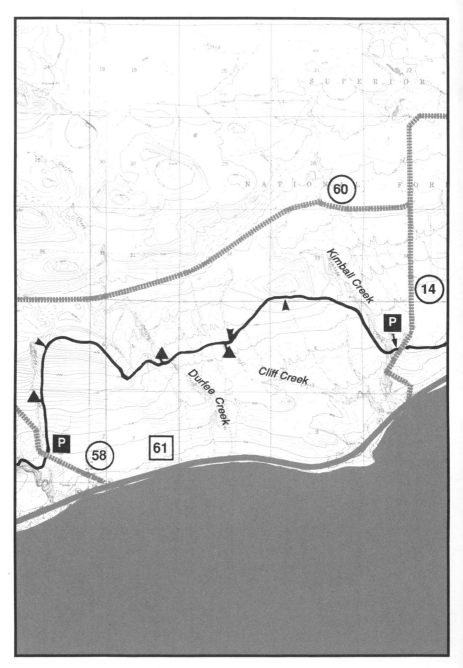

COUNTY RD 58 TO KADUNCE RIVER

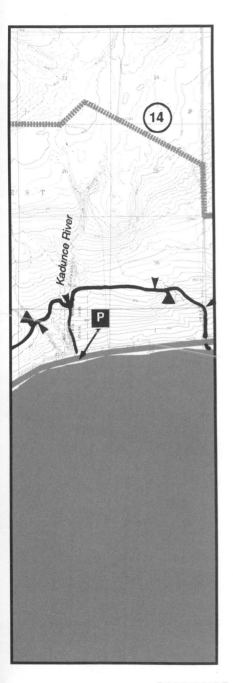

Unusual Forests

Most of Minnesota's Arrowhead is boreal forest, with typical stands of evergreen spruce and balsam fir, and deciduous birch and aspen communities. This boreal type is quite common along the Trail. Having all this similar forest makes the exceptions all the more dramatic. Watch for unusual stands of black ash, a species prized by basketmakers, in well-drained lowland areas. The high parts of the Trail wind through occasional stands of oak in the southern half, although by the time the Trail reaches Cook County, most of the oaks are gone. Other unusual tree species to watch out for include ironwood, basswood and American elm.

4.1 (5.1)
Cliff Creek crossing
The last of the many creeks in this section. This plank is longer than the earlier ones. Now woods get more mixed, with birch, aspen and fir. Lake comes into view, maples appear, and the sharp, red rhyolite returns underfoot.

> **Cliff Creek campsite**
> Location: west side of Cliff Creek
> Tent spaces: 2-3
> Water: from creek

5.1 (4.1)
Scrub-oak overlook
Expansive view of Lake, now including Red Cliff. On SHT look for the unusual small oak trees, then spruce plantation and large (30" diameter) aspens. SHT begins to follow Kimball Creek, then crosses it and meets the Kimball Creek Trail junction. SHT then crosses a tributary and climbs steep steps.

6.8 (2.4)
Cook Co. Rd. 14
SHT crosses road and climbs through cutover area, then passes under powerline before entering a fir/birch/aspen woods. A view of Lake, then SHT descends. Look for bunchberry and thimbleberry (with galls that look like swollen kneecaps). SHT crosses a couple of footpaths and a small opening. Path is mostly rock here. SHT descends stone steps to creek.

7.9 (1.3)
Crow Creek
This stream has the steep rock walls typical of Kadunce River country visible upstream from the bridge. Campsite under construction as of 1992. SHT climbs out of creek bed, crosses a footpath, then another narrow steep canyon, the west fork of the Kadunce River. Watch for bearing tree near SHT right before crossing Kadunce River.

8.5 (0.7)
Kadunce River

On far side of bridge, go downstream on spectacular spur trail to Hwy. 61. Spur follows river until river drops into gorge, then rejoins river after gorge. The river itself is a wonderful upstream hike. Hikers will get wet up to their thighs. This should be attempted only when the water is very low because four waterfalls must be ascended using all fours. The canyon is very deep yet only about 8' wide in places.

9.2 (0.0)
Kadunce River wayside on Hwy. 61

Kadunce River to Magney State Park

Start (End)
Kadunce Creek Wayside on Hwy. 61

End (Start)
Judge C.R. Magney State Park

Length of trail section
10.0 miles

Safety concerns
• Trail near cliff edge at times along Kadunce River

Access and parking
Kadunce River:
Nearest Hwy. 61 milepost: 119

Secondary road name and number: none

Parking spaces available: 11 spaces available, no overnight

Lakewalk:
Nearest Hwy. 61 milepost: 120.2 at west end, 121.6 at east end

Secondary road name and number: none

Parking spaces available: 6 on lakeside, officially no overnight

Facilities
At starting trailhead (furthest southwest): none

Designated campsites on this section of trail: one — near un-named creek

Synopsis
This is an exciting section of the SHT, since it is the only part which is directly on the Lake Superior shoreline. It also passes many different stages of succession following logging in the area, and some classic North Shore river gorges, including that of the Kadunce River.

Mile-by-mile description

0.0 (10.0)
Kadunce Wayside
This spectacular spur trail begins climbing almost immediately along the edge of the Kadunce River gorge, which is pocked by occasional "swirl caves" created at various stages of the gorge's creation. Spur begins to level out momentarily where it meets the main SHT at a bridge crossing the Kadunce River.

0.7 (9.3)
Footbridge over Kadunce River
Spur trail joins main SHT here. Crossing bridge, SHT leads southwest to Co. Rd. 58. SHT turns away from bridge, then climbs hill and follows river upstream past cascades, then climbs again and leaves river. Forest changes from birch and fir to dense, relatively younger aspen stand. SHT crosses an old grassy logging roadbed and then two footpaths.

2.0 (8.0)
Blueberry Overlook
Follow rock cairns through open area which leads to overlook with expansive view of Lake Superior. Just beyond overlook a short spur trail leads to campsite. SHT crosses stream and enters dark woods, then a recently logged area. Look for an old red pine stump that is a "nurse log" to a young birch. SHT then enters another logged area replanted with spruce, with large white pines left standing. SHT descends log ladder and passes many raspberry patches in a 350 acre clearcut.

> **Blueberry Overlook campsite**
> Location: down short spur trail between overlook and small stream
> Tent spaces: 1-2
> Water: from stream - unreliable

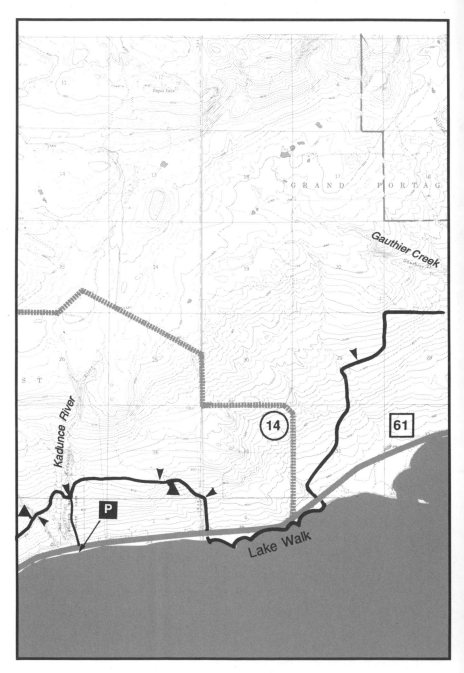

Gauthier Creek

14

61

Kadunce River

Lake Walk

P

GRAND PORTAG

S T

Fergus Lake

11

12

14

13

18

17

18

19

20

26

24

26

25

30

29

28

35

36

31

32

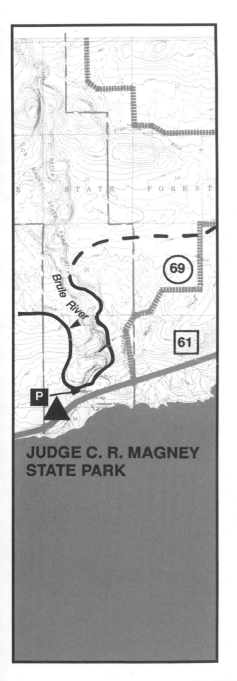

**JUDGE C. R. MAGNEY
STATE PARK**

Pebble Beaches

A beach must have both a source of rock particles and wave action to deposit and move the particles. Beaches continually change in reaction to changes in the waves from storm to calm to storm. Some of the smaller beaches on the North Shore are made of rocks ripped from the nearby bedrock ledges; larger beaches are made possible where the waves have access to more easily-eroded glacial deposits. The long, low beaches between Grand Marais and Hovland are made both from local volcanic rhyolite, which breaks up into easily erodible chips or shingles, and reworked older beach deposits from the Nipissing stage of Lake Superior, about 5000 years ago, when the Lake was slightly higher and the beaches were on the other side of what is now the highway. Can you find any agates? They might have been brought by the ice sheet from Isle Royale or Canada.

2.7 (7.3)
Gravel road
SHT crosses road (note SHT mileage sign), then descends through scrubby woods, dense young aspen stand and mixed woods.

3.2 (6.8)
Hwy. 61, west end of Lakewalk
SHT is marked on both sides of Hwy. 61. SHT follows shore of Lake on a soft pebble beach. This is the only part of the SHT on Lake Superior. Here one can literally touch the many moods of this great Lake. Lakeshore camping is available, though there is no official campsite and minimum impact camping must be implemented. Notice the different surge levels up the beach from storms and wind, especially the unimposed northeast winds. Look for bog areas between beach and Hwy. 61 – good spring birding, as birds use shoreline for navigation. SHT turns inland just past a very small rock island barely off shore.

4.8 (5.2)
Hwy. 61, east end of Lakewalk
SHT passes large birches and passes under powerline and through mixed woods along Hane Creek. Cross stream on small wood bridge after passing through low areas and logged sections. SHT eventually climbs and passes large cedar and white pine and overlooks of water-falls and pools below. Caution: SHT comes close to cliff edge. SHT crosses stream on log planking, ascends through mature aspen, then levels out. This section passes through a portion of private land. Please respect the owner's rights; stay on trail and do not camp or build fires.

6.2 (3.8)
Gravel pit road
SHT crosses several cutover open areas with varied woods in between. Look for blueberries in open sections. For approximately 1.5 miles the SHT follows the straight borderline of private property, past Lake views and mature pines. SHT crosses old road bed upon exiting

another section of private land and shortly passes bearing tree and survey line, then follows Gauthier Creek.

9.1 (0.9)
Junction with state park trail
As the trail begins to pull away from Gauthier Creek, the SHT merges with state park trail. Stay right on this grassy trail.

10.0 (0.0)
Judge C.R. Magney State Park trailhead
SHT enters parking lot located just north of state park campground.

Magney State Park to Arrowhead Trail

Start (End)
Judge C.R. Magney State Park

End (Start)
Arrowhead Trail

This section of the SHT is scheduled for construction in the spring of 1993. When complete, it will be approximately 9 miles in length, and will follow park trails past the Devil's Kettle, and continue up the Brule River for another mile. The SHT will then leave the river valley and wander through mixed forest of old growth hardwoods. It will cross the Flute Reed River and include many breathtaking views of Lake Superior.

Judge C.R. Magney State Park

Judge C.R. Magney State Park is named after the former Minnesota Supreme Court Justice Clarence R. Magney. A strong advocate of Minnesota state parks, he was instrumental in establishing eleven parks and waysides along the North Shore. This park was established in 1957 to preserve three waterfalls on the Brule River: the Lower Falls, the Upper Falls, and the Devil's Kettle.

The Devil's Kettle was named appropriately. A large rock juts out and splits the river in two. The east branch drops 50 feet to a deep gorge and pool. The west branch plunges into a huge pothole and, according to legend, disappears forever. 4514 acres in size, today the park remains relatively undeveloped with six miles of hiking trails, 36 rustic campsites, and one backpack site.

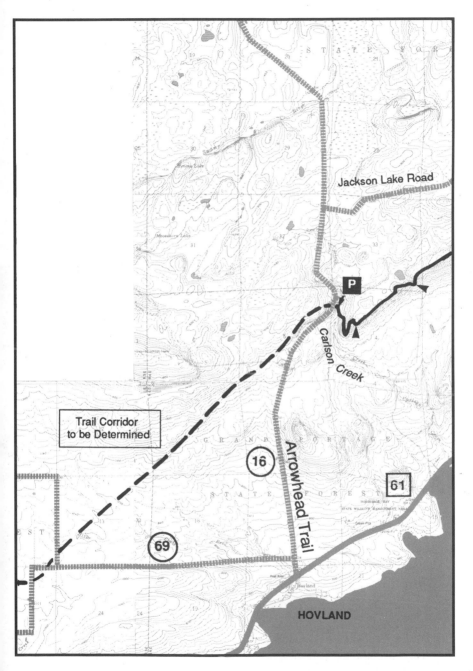

Jackson Lake Road

P

Carlson Creek

Trail Corridor
to be Determined

16

Arrowhead Trail

61

69

HOVLAND

MAGNEY TO ARROWHEAD TRAIL   163

Arrowhead Trail to Jackson Lake Road

Start (End)
Arrowhead Trail (Cook Co. Rd. 16) north of Hovland

End (Start)
Jackson Lake Rd.

Length of trail section
5.1 miles

Safety concerns
• Blowdowns in spruce-fir forests may obscure the trail

Access and parking
West end:
Nearest Hwy. 61 milepost: 128.9

Secondary road name and number: Arrowhead Trail (Cook Co. Rd. 16)

Etc: Follow Arrowhead Trail 3.3 miles. Trailhead is on right. No official parking lot as of 1992, but room in pull-off for 2-3 cars. Overnight okay.

East end:
Continue on Arrowhead Trail 1.2 miles past western end

trailhead, or 4.5 total miles from Hwy. 61. Turn right on Jackson Lake Rd. 3.0 miles on Jackson Lake Rd. to trailhead on right in a cedar swamp. Park on roadside. Caution: there are many logging trucks on this road, so park well off the roadway if possible.

Facilities
At starting trailhead: none

Designated campsites on this section of the SHT: none

Synopsis
This farthest–north section of the SHT is home to the ghost of the woodland caribou. Moss-covered rocks and lichen-draped trees give this land a true boreal feel. Experience the variety as the SHT winds from open rocky ridges with wide views of the Lake and Isle Royale, into dark forests and quiet backwaters. One-half of this section follows an open rocky ridge, with nearly continual views.

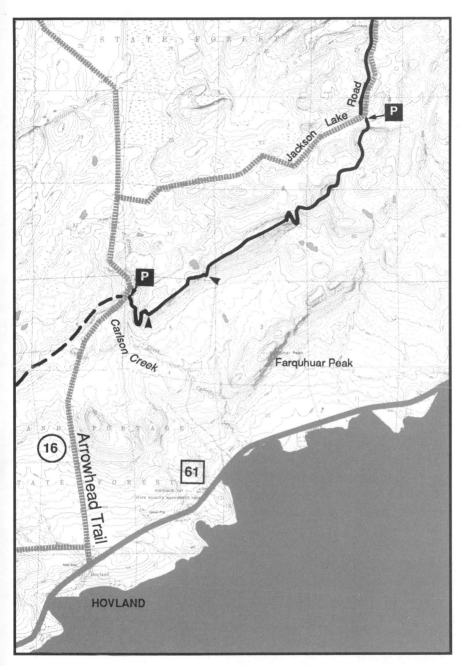

ARROWHEAD TRAIL TO JACKSON LAKE RD

Mile-by-mile description

0.0 (5.1)
Pull-off on Arrowhead Trail
SHT departs from right side of lot, nearly parallel to the road, descending steeply through aspen and fir to Carlson Creek. SHT crosses creek on 15' bridge, continues along creek through alder before climbing past some large spruce and up through an unusual older balsam fir stand.

0.6 (4.5)
Southwest end of ridgetop
From the first view through some young aspens, the SHT meanders along this ridgeline for 1.5 miles. Cairns lead the way through mixed spruce, fir and aspen forest as the views keep getting better. Look for Isle Royale over 20 miles away. Before descending to creek, SHT enters private land. Watch for beaver meadow as SHT nears creek.

1.6 (3.5)
Creek crossing
This is a small creek, crossed on mossy stepping stones. SHT skirts east edge of the beaver meadow, then climbs back to the ridgetop through dead and dying fir. Occasional large spruce show what this forest might have been like before logging or disease. In a grassy opening, faint trail goes down to homesteads below, then SHT returns to open rocky vistas, including a 180° overlook and a narrow ridge with seasonal views to both sides. SHT descends steeply from ridge into a valley, with nice views of beaver pond and Lake below. Another dark forest, once the habitat of the woodland caribou, before the SHT meets the un-named creek where the water appears to caress the moss-covered boulders.

3.2 (1.9)
Creek crossing
SHT crosses this well-flowing creek on a split-log footbridge, near a couple of black ash, then climbs east side of creek and, like the previous creek crossing, follows the edge of the beaver meadow. SHT climbs through a relatively mature mixed birch forest.

3.9 (1.2)
"Hellacious Overlook"
Steep climb rewards hikers with a wide view to Lake, Isle Royale, beaver meadows below, etc. SHT continues along ridgetop, with more views to the northeast, then descends steeply past dead and dying fir, into a wet area with alder and ash. Forest here is older and more varied than western end of section. SHT gradually climbs through aspen and birch and diseased fir, then descends steeply into a cedar swamp and across a corduroy walkway to the road.

5.1 (0.0)
Jackson Lake Rd.
This is the northeast terminus of the SHT as of Fall '92.

Jackson Lake Road to Canada

Synopsis

Although the SHT ends at the Jackson Lake Rd. as of fall 1992, there is much more hiking beyond. Eventually, the SHT will connect with the Border Route Trail, where one can put a foot into the Pigeon River and toss a stone into Canada. The Border Route Trail extends westward from the upper stretches of the Jackson Lake Rd. for approximately 84 miles. It traverses the most rugged section of the Boundary Waters Canoe Area Wilderness, offering views which match in splendor those of the SHT. At the western terminus of the Border Route Trail, on the Gunflint Trail highway, the Kekekabic Trail continues westward another 40 miles to the Fernberg Rd. near Ely.

Your dreams need not end with the Kekekabic Trail. A trail is in the works which will link Ely with Grand Rapids, where the dedicated hiker can join the developing North Country Trail which links Maine and North Dakota. Happy hiking!

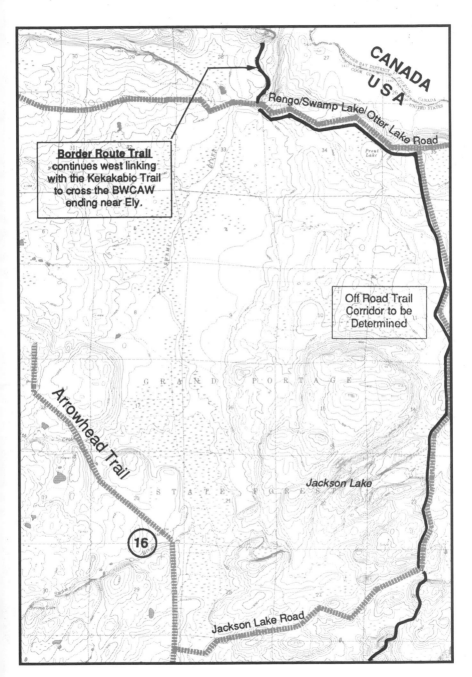

Border Route Trail continues west linking with the Kekakabic Trail to cross the BWCAW ending near Ely.

CANADA
U S A

Rengo/Swamp Lake/Otter Lake Road

Off Road Trail Corridor to be Determined

Arrowhead Trail

G R A N D   P O R T A G E

S T A T E   F O R E S T

Jackson Lake

(16)

Jackson Lake Road

Suggested Hikes

Although each section of the Superior Hiking Trail has its own charms, certain of the sections have proven themselves to be excellent introductions to the Trail's varied character. Following are a few of the many day hike possibilities which hikers from all over the world are finding to be the best in the Midwest.

Split Rock River

Park your car at the highway wayside near the mouth of the river. A 4.5 mile round-trip hike leads up the very scenic river past numerous falls, cascades and pools. The return route crosses the river and heads to a high overlook. Follow the ski trail back to the highway near your car.

Bean and Bear Lakes

Park on Penn Boulevard in Silver Bay. The Trail leads northeastward 6.4 miles round trip to the vertical cliffs above Bean and Bear Lakes.

Mount Trudee

Park at the Tettegouche State Park Trail Center. Hike approximately 6 miles round trip to Mount Trudee. Rugged clifftops overlook Palisade Creek Valley.

Carlton Peak

Park at the Britton Peak trailhead at the crest of the hill on the Sawbill Trail (County Road 2) above Tofte. Hike a short four miles round trip to the summit of Carlton Peak, a bald dome of granitic rock with sweeping views.

Oberg Mountain

Access is from Forest Service Road 336 near Tofte. The 2.5 mile loop to the top of Oberg Mountain has 9 overlooks (including the view seen on the cover of this book).

Lutsen Mountains

Ride the Lutsen ski area gondola to the top of Moose Mountain, over 1000 feet above Lake Superior. Then walk a moderately strenuous 3.6 miles on the Trail back to your car through a forest of maples.

Devil Track Canyon

Park on County Road 58 northeast of Grand Marais at a small stream crossing about 1 mile uphill from Highway 61. Walk approximately 1/2 mile to the deepest canyon in Minnesota. Walk 2 to 6 miles along the canyon rim before returning.

Kadunce River

A very short spur leads from the Kadunce River wayside on Highway 61 between Grand Marais and Hovland to the Superior Hiking Trail. The deep Kadunce River gorge is a "must see."

Lake Superior Walk

Just southwest of Judge C.R. Magney State Park, the Superior Hiking Trail crosses Highway 61 and follows a Lake Superior cobblestone beach for 1.5 miles.

Towns Along the Superior Hiking Trail

The communities listed are those accessible from the Superior Hiking Trail. The population figures are provided to suggest the extent of facilities hikers may expect to find.

Community	Zip	Population	Services	Medical	Hwy. 61 Milepost
Two Harbors	55616	3651	M, L, G, C, LM, O	Hospital	26.1
Castle Danger	—	—	M, LG, L	—	37.1
Beaver Bay	55601	147	M, L, LG, LM	—	51.0
Silver Bay	55614	1894	M, L, G, LM	Clinic	54.3
Illgen City	—	—	L	—	59.3
Finland	55603	—	M, L, G	—	—
Schroeder	55613	—	M, L, G, C	—	79.0
Tofte	55615	250	M, L, LG, O	—	82.6
Lutsen	55612	—	M, L, G	—	91.7
Grand Marais	55604	1171	M, L, G, C, LM, O	Hospital	109.5

Services

M = meals
L = lodging
G = groceries
LG = limited groceries
C = camping
LM = laundromat
O = outfitting supplies

Emergencies
911 in all three counties

Mail
Hiker's mail should be marked "General Delivery – Hold for hiker on Superior Hiking Trail." Post office hours vary.

Additional information for hikers
• Superior Hiking Trail Association, PO Box 4, Two Harbors, MN 55616 (218) 834-4436

• Lutsen-Tofte Tourism Association, Tofte, MN 55614

• Tip of the Arrowhead Association, Grand Marais, MN 55604

• Turner Bus Lines, 1220 Commerce St., Thunder Bay, Ontario P7C 4V5 (807) 475-4500; *Providing daily service to the towns along the North Shore*

• US Forest Service: Tofte Ranger Station (218) 663-7280; Grand Marais Ranger Station (218) 327-1750

• Minnesota State Parks: DNR Parks, 500 Lafayette Rd., St. Paul, MN 55155 (612) 296-6157 or (800) 652-9747

A Final Note:

The trouble is, we're tempted to think that a guided description can really describe and guide. Of course, no matter how well done, it cannot. It depends on what we're looking for.

The Superior Hiking Trail leads us from the mountain tops to the valley floors, to the deep woods and the cascading rivers. A guide can describe a rocky overlook at such and so, but it cannot tell whether it's fogged in or not.

And who's to say whether we find in the fog the mystery of the north woods, or whether we find disappointment in not seeing farther?

I'd like to pick a defining experience, a place and time on the Trail where it all came together for me in some kind of mystical peak experience. The retelling of this, I believe, could show the true value of the Trail. But would it really? We can wax poetically all we want about the North Shore and the ridgeline, and it will all be true. The truth is, the value we experience depends on what we're seeking.

Instead, for me, faces come to mind. It is the faces and personalities of all those who brought the Trail to life with sweat and good humor. It is Mark, Duane, Bob, Cory, Toivo, Neil, Harry, Stormy, and forty others who did the actual work of trail building. It is John, Tom, Bill, and Anne who, by the force of their character, willed the Trail into existence.

For this trail to be really worthwhile, it should be more than just fun. It should heighten our awareness and appreciation of all that is natural.

It should make us realize our place in the diverse complex web that is the land. With a little luck and a little help it might, for a few of us. And that would be worthwhile.

— TOM PETERSON

Join the Superior Hiking Trail Association!

APPLICATION FOR MEMBERSHIP OR RENEWAL
(Note: Memberships run for one year from receipt of application)

Membership Categories:
(Check type of membership desired)

___ Student/Senior	$15	___ Individual	$20
___ Family	30	___ Youth organization/	
___ Supporting	100	Non-profit	40
___ Life Member	500	___ Donation $_____	

CORPORATE

___ Contributing	$50	___ Sustaining	$500
___ Supporting	100	___ Patron	1,000
___ Donation $_____			

Enclosed is $ _____ for (check below):

❏ New membership
❏ Renewal (Member number _____)

Name: _____

Address: _____

_____

Home Tel: _____ Work Tel: _____

*The Superior Hiking Trail Association is composed of volunteers.
To accomplish our goals, we need the active involvement of our members.*

I am interested in helping the Superior Hiking Trail Association through:

___ Constructing trails	___ Maintaining trails
___ Fund-raising	___ Promotion/Publicity/
___ Programs (leading hikes)	Marketing
___ Group presentations	___ Art/Photography
___ Special skills: _____	
___ Liaison with other organizations	
(name of group _____)	

Mail to Superior Hiking Trail Assn., PO Box 4, Two Harbors, MN 55616